I0605471

A gift for
From
Date

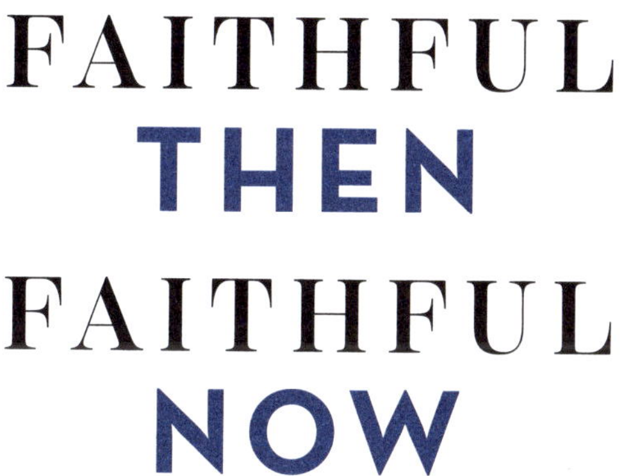

Faithful Then Faithful Now

Unlock Ancient Wisdom for a Confident Life Today

A 40-Day Devotional

ZONDERVAN

Faithful Then, Faithful Now

Published by Zondervan, 3950 Sparks Drive SE, Suite 101, Grand Rapids, MI 49546, USA. Zondervan is a registered trademark of The Zondervan Corporation, L.L.C., a wholly owned subsidiary of HarperCollins Christian Publishing, Inc.

Requests for information should be addressed to customercare@harpercollins.com.

HarperCollins Publishers, Macken House, 39/40 Mayor Street Upper, Dublin 1, D01 C9W8, Ireland (https://www.harpercollins.com)

Art direction: Patti Evans
Interior design: Lori Lynch

ISBN 978-0-310-46715-1 (HC)
ISBN 978-0-310-46717-5 (audiobook)
ISBN 978-0-310-46716-8 (eBook)

Printed in Malaysia
25 26 27 28 29 OFF 10 9 8 7 6 5 4 3 2 1

Contents

Adam and Eve

UNFAITHFUL HUMANS, FAITHFUL GOD

READ GENESIS 3

As we receive the sacrament of communion in our churches on Sundays, we often hear about how God faithfully kept covenant with us even when we humans fell into sin. God pursued us, covered our sin, and gave Christ to secure our salvation at the cross. The amazing faithfulness of God sustains us through every season of life.

We see this from the very beginning, with the first two humans, Adam and Eve. God created them in his image, giving them the special task of caring for his creation (Genesis 1:26–27). Archaeologists point out that ancient temples often had "images," or statues of gods, placed inside them.[1] The picture in Genesis is that all creation is God's temple, and humans are his living images within it.[2] These first things we learn about this pair are still at the core of what it means to be human today: We carry the image of God, and we care for creation.

Adam and Eve lived in the garden of Eden, in harmony with God, with the world, and with each other. Sadly, this state of innocence and harmony was short-lived. One day, the Serpent tempted Eve to eat from the one tree God had forbidden them to eat from, the Tree of Knowledge of Good and Evil. After being tempted, Eve took and ate from the tree and shared the fruit with her husband (Genesis 3:6). The blame isn't on Eve alone; Scripture is clear that Adam was "with her" during this encounter, and he was the one who first received the prohibition from God not to eat from the tree (2:16–17).

With this act of disobedience and unfaithfulness, Adam and Eve brought sin into the world. The harmony in their relationship with creation was broken, as was their relationship with God and each other (3:16–19).

It may seem strange to begin a forty-day journey on faithfulness with this story of human *un*faithfulness. However, Adam and Eve's story

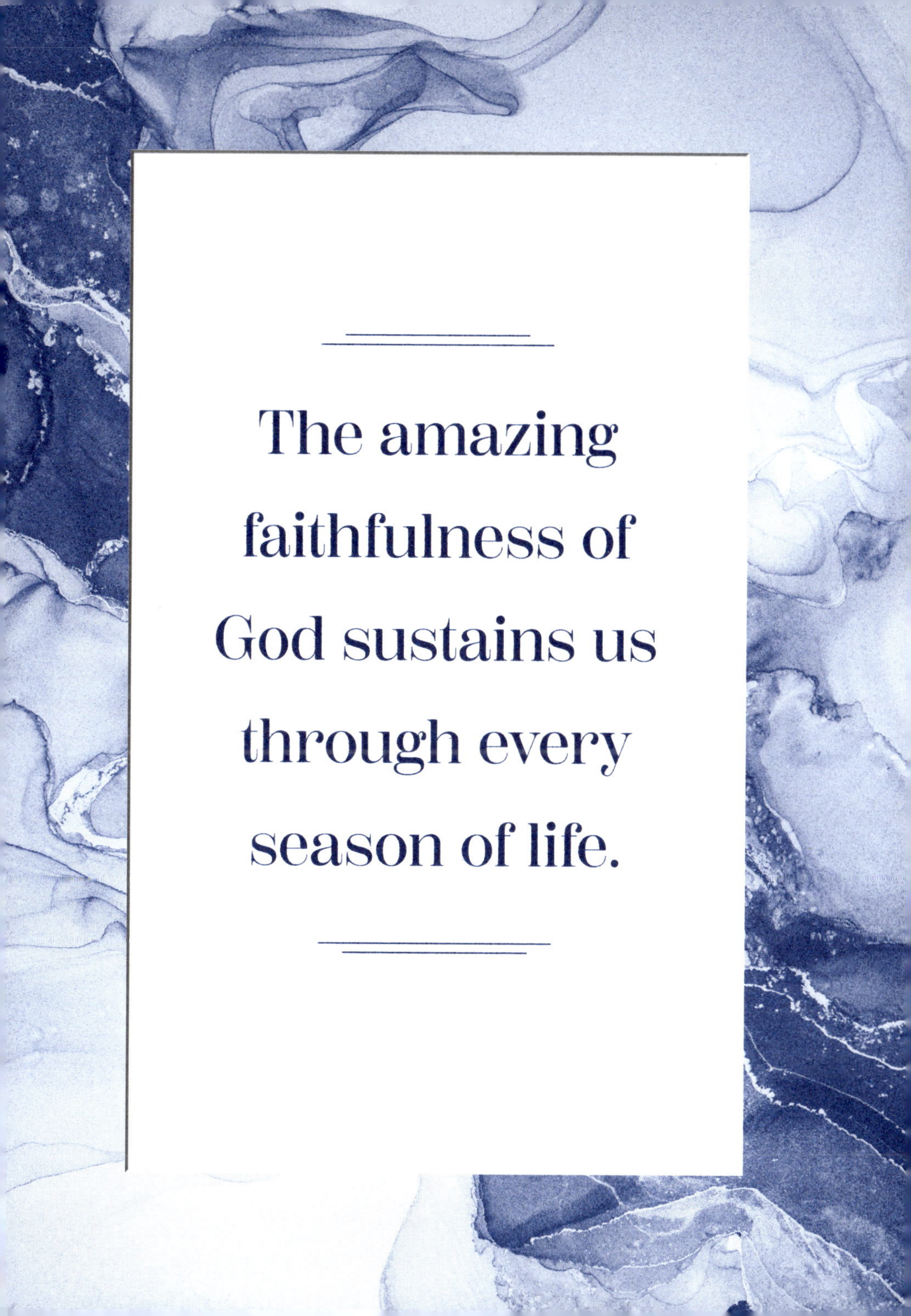
The amazing faithfulness of God sustains us through every season of life.

shows faithfulness of the most important kind. Yes, they disobeyed God, but God nevertheless showed amazing grace and faithfulness toward them. He pursued them (Genesis 3:9) and covered them in their shame with animal skin (v. 21).

God's faithfulness to his people, even in the face of sin and failure, is a deep and sure comfort in life. God is the faithful one in this story, and that's wonderful news—for Adam and Eve at the very beginning, and for you and me today. We are still made in God's image, so by God's grace and Spirit, we can mirror God's faithfulness. In fact, faithfulness is a fruit of the Spirit, and it looks like living reliable, steadfast lives of commitment because of what we believe. This means honoring commitments to God and to the people in our lives and honoring our responsibility toward all creation.

A life of faithfulness displays God's love to the world. When you live out your response to God's faithfulness to you, you begin to restore what was broken through sin.

Today, as you begin this forty-day journey, pray for God's grace and guidance as you seek to live faithfully in response to his faithfulness to you.

DAY 2

Noah

A MAN WHO DIDN'T FIT IN

READ GENESIS 6:9–22

Psychologists have studied the ways humans are prone to peer pressure. We want to fit in with the group. In one psychological experiment, subjects were presented with a line and then shown three more lines to compare to the first line. One of the three comparison lines was the same length as the original line, while the other two were either much longer or much shorter. Researchers then asked, "Which of these three lines is most similar to the first line?" The experiment was designed in such a way that the correct answer was obvious. The alarming result was that when there were actors in the room with the subject, posing as additional subjects themselves, and those actors all picked the wrong answer, most of the study's subjects picked the wrong answer as well—in fact, 75 percent chose an obviously wrong answer at least once in order to conform to the crowd! For most people, fitting in was more important than giving the answer they knew to be true.[3]

Sometimes it feels as though the world is falling apart, that this present moment is worse than any the world has ever experienced. While concern about the state of the world is valid, Genesis 6 depicts a world far worse than ours today. According to the Bible, the world at this point in creation had become so corrupt that "every inclination of the thoughts of the human heart was only evil all the time" (v. 5). Violence and sin soaked the fabric of society. Humanity spiraled into such pervasive evil that God regretted he had made humans and considered wiping them out (v. 7).

There was one man, however, who was different: Noah. His name means "comfort" (Genesis 5:29). In stark contrast to the evil around him, Noah is described as a man who was righteous and blameless, and his story is a ray of hope in a world of moral corruption (6:9).

The Bible says Noah "walked faithfully with God" (v. 9). That language reveals relationship. Noah lived a life conscious of God's presence with him. He was close to God. Imagine the moral and spiritual strength it took for Noah to live faithfully in a world so full of corruption. This is a strength that depends on God's grace working within a person; yet believers also have a responsibility to walk in step with God's will and guidance. Noah faithfully walked in step, even when every single person around him rejected God.

Noah's faithfulness wasn't only on display in how he resisted participating in the evil around him, though. He also showed faithful obedience to God by doing what God told him to do, even when it sounded absurd. God told Noah to build an enormous ark for himself, his family, and a multitude of animals (6:14). Noah's faithful obedience demonstrated his absolute trust in God. Even when God's instructions seemed to make no sense and would make Noah look odd in the eyes of those around him, Noah obeyed.

His two qualities of faithfulness—nonconformity to the world and obedience to God's instructions—rise from the pages of Scripture as a challenge to God's children today.

It's all too easy to compromise what's right for the sake of fitting in. In the face of this danger, we need to remember Noah and remain righteous, no matter what the people around us do or think. Even when God's instructions sound odd, or when obedience to God makes us stand out in uncomfortable ways, we can know that faithfulness to God is what matters most.

Paul's words in Romans 12 challenge us to be like Noah, resisting the sinful and harmful patterns we see around us and instead living a Christlike and God-glorifying life. Paul wrote, "Do not conform to the pattern of this world, but be transformed by the renewing of your mind.

Even when
God's
instructions
seemed to make
no sense . . .
Noah obeyed.

Then you will be able to test and approve what God's will is—his good, pleasing and perfect will" (v. 2). Living in and obeying that will, even when we're the only ones doing so, is the path to the faithful and fulfilling life to which God calls us in Christ Jesus.

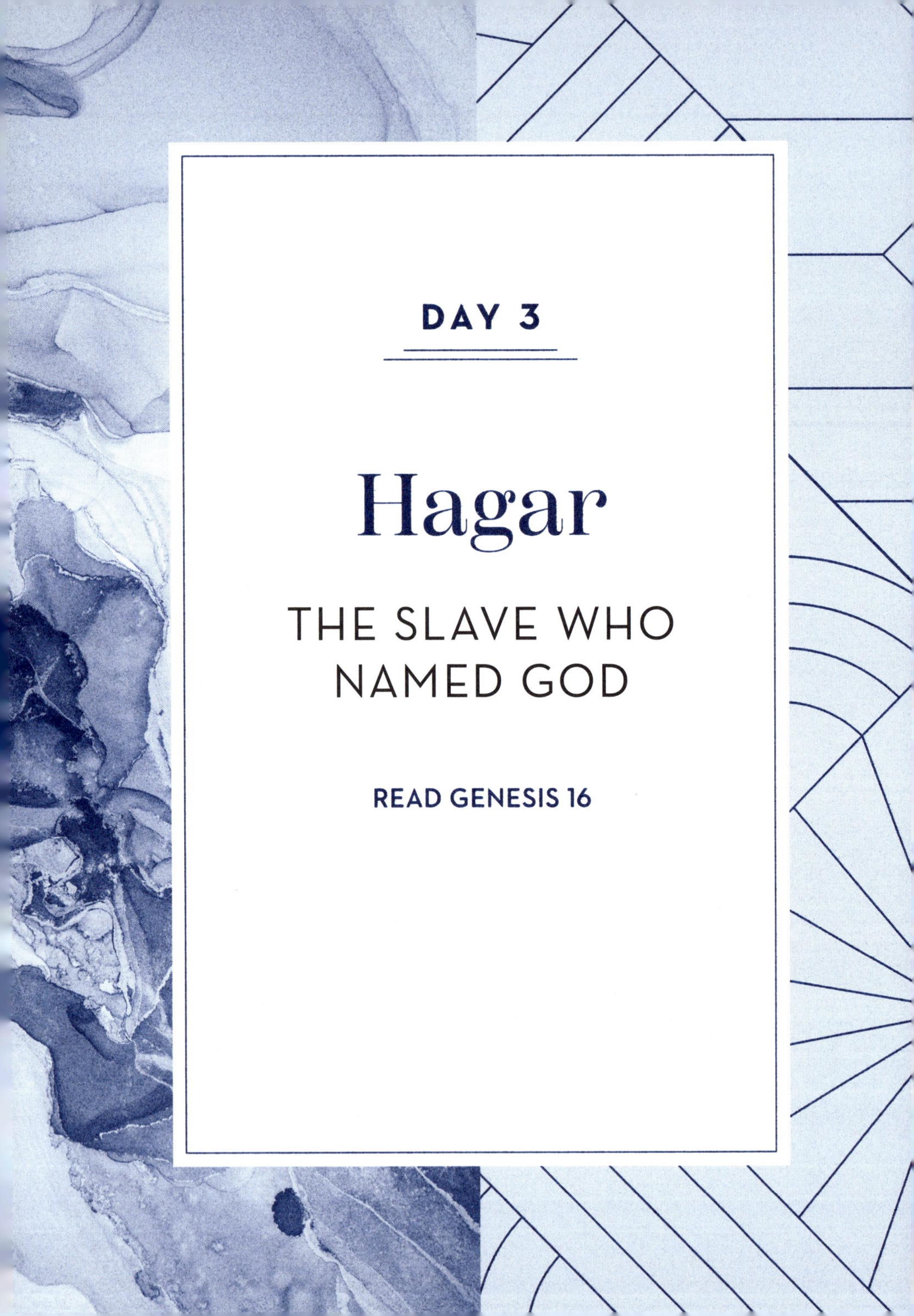

DAY 3

Hagar

THE SLAVE WHO NAMED GOD

READ GENESIS 16

As we explore the stories in the Bible, we discover how complex the characters in it really are. Many are marginalized or oppressed, and they often show amazing strength and faith in God.

Hagar is the first of these unlikely faith heroes we'll cover in this journey, a woman who, despite her position in society, displayed a powerful trust in God.

Hagar's story is not without tension that might make us uncomfortable. For one thing, Abram and Sarai—the couple we'll focus on in tomorrow's reading—do not look so good in the Hagar episode. Hagar was Sarai's Egyptian slave, presumably acquired while Abram and Sarai were in Egypt (Genesis 12:10–20).

You see, this couple had a problem. God had promised Abram he would make a great nation out of him, with descendants who would bless all people (vv. 1–3). But he and Sarai were unable to have children (11:30). So Sarai devised a plan to use Hagar to build a family for herself. Since Hagar was Sarai's slave, any children Hagar bore would belong to Sarai.

That's the proposition Sarai made to Abram. "Sleep with my slave; perhaps I can build a family through her" (16:2). Abram consented. Notice that the Bible is silent on Hagar's feelings about this, at least until she became pregnant. Knowing the child in her womb would not be considered hers, Hagar grew to despise Sarai.

Sarai complained to Abram about the conflicts arising with Hagar, blaming him for what happened (v. 5). Abram told Sarai to handle the situation however she thought best.

Let's pause to see something noteworthy about how Abram and Sarai spoke about Hagar. They didn't use her name. Instead, they called her "my slave" (vv. 2, 5) and "your slave" (v. 6). The Bible gives the impression that they saw Hagar only as a possession, not a person.

What tragically follows is that Sarai mistreated Hagar to the point that pregnant Hagar fled into the wilderness. She chose almost certain death in the unforgiving desert over staying with Sarai. There in the wilderness, however, God showed up. And the first word the angel of the Lord spoke to Hagar, in vivid contrast to Abram and Sarai, was her name: Hagar (v. 8). The angel showed Hagar a spring of water and told her to return to Sarai. Interestingly, Hagar's name means "forsaken," but this story shows us that she was not forsaken by God!

Here is another tension that might make us uncomfortable: God's angel told Hagar to return to Sarai and "submit to her" (v. 9). But at the same time, God made Hagar an amazing promise—one that echoes the powerful promise given to Abram: "I will increase your descendants so much that they will be too numerous to count" (v. 10). Further, God's messenger told Hagar her son would be named Ishmael, meaning "God hears," because "the LORD has heard of your misery" (v. 11).

All this brings us to Hagar's powerful act. She named God: "You are the God who sees me" (v. 13), or in Hebrew, El Roi. She named God based on what God had done for her: He saw her, heard her, and cared for her in her misery.

The Bible gives us many names and descriptions for God. The book of Psalms, for example, is full of vivid metaphors and titles for God. He is a "righteous judge" (7:11), "helper of the fatherless" (10:14), "refuge" of the poor (14:6), our "strength" (18:1), our "Rock" (19:14), "our refuge and strength, an ever-present help" (46:1). Describing God and recalling what he has done for us can and should be an important part of our prayers.

As you reflect on Hagar's story, think about what name you would give God, based on how God has shown his love and mercy to you.

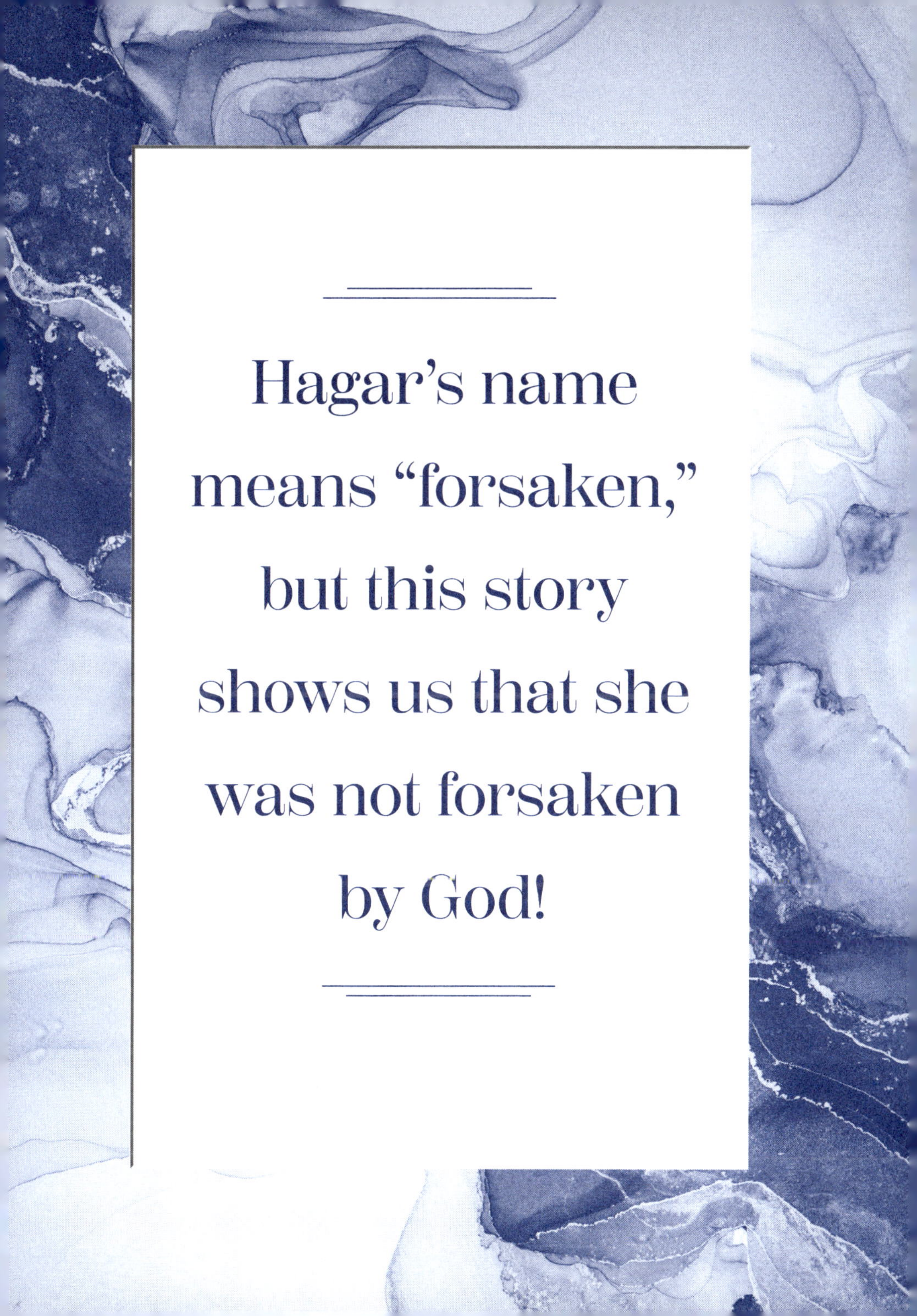
Hagar's name
means "forsaken,"
but this story
shows us that she
was not forsaken
by God!

Describe what God has done for you. Praise him for his faithful love to you, in bad times and good, sharing with him honestly what that name means to you.

Remember that God knows you by name. He loves you, he sees you, and he hears you.

DAY 4

Abraham and Sarah

THE PAIR WHO SERVED GOD LUNCH

READ GENESIS 18:1–15

God appeared or spoke to Abraham multiple times, but the episode in Genesis 18 may be the most intriguing. In this passage, God showed up in human form. In fact, three men came to see Abraham. These three men appeared to be God and two angels.

Abraham's response to God was immediate. He hurried toward the travelers and bowed, asking them to stay and relax before continuing their journey. When the men accepted his invitation, Abraham set out quickly to prepare a huge feast, with the help of his wife, Sarah. Abraham asked Sarah to take three *seah*s (in total, probably around sixty pounds) of the "finest flour" to knead into dough and bake into bread. In the meantime, Abraham prepared a choice calf and got some curds and milk.

We can see that Abraham's meal was not a light continental breakfast. The size of this meal seems entirely disproportionate to the occasion. Three men showed up to Abraham's tent, and he and Sarah proceeded to prepare a feast. This was a banquet, with enough food for the travelers to take leftovers with them if they wished.

Though it may seem like a small thing, radical hospitality is an important way believers can live out their faith. Quite likely with the story of Abraham and the three visitors in mind, the writer of Hebrews said, "Do not forget to show hospitality to strangers, for by so doing some people have shown hospitality to angels without knowing it" (13:2).

Yet our motivation for hospitality should not be that we hope the folks we serve are angels in disguise (though that is a fantastic thought!). Our kindness should be part and parcel of living out the Christian faith with other people. Recall what Jesus said about those who feed the hungry, dress the naked, give water to the thirsty, care for the sick, and visit the imprisoned: "Whatever you did for one of the least of these brothers

The kingdom of God is characterized by generosity and care for others.

and sisters of mine, you did for me" (Matthew 25:40). How we treat others—especially the marginalized—is a reflection of what we really think of Christ himself. Our love for Christ should overflow into kindness and hospitality for those around us.

Jesus himself made a veiled reference to the story of Abraham, Sarah, and the three visitors. In Matthew 13:33, he said, "The kingdom of heaven is like yeast that a woman took and mixed into about sixty pounds of flour until it worked all through the dough." Where the Bible says "about sixty pounds," the Greek text says *tria sata,* three measures totaling about sixty pounds. Here Christ connects the hospitality of Sarah and Abraham to what the kingdom of heaven is like! The kingdom of God is characterized by generosity and care for others.

Consider where there are opportunities for you to practice hospitality and generosity in your life. Is there a ministry at a local prison you could volunteer with? A mentoring program for elementary students at a nearby school? Maybe you could visit some elderly people from your church community who are now confined to a nursing home. Perhaps you could bless a couple with young children by offering to babysit (or pay for a babysitter) while they go out and spend some time together. Be creatively hospitable! As Romans 12:13 says, "Share with the Lord's people who are in need. Practice hospitality." When you follow that invitation, you echo the faithfulness of Abraham and Sarah. As Christ reminds us, practicing radical hospitality gives the world a picture of the kingdom of heaven. What an exciting invitation!

DAY 5

Jacob

THE PENITENT TRICKSTER

READ GENESIS 33:1–11

There is no grudge more bitter than one between family members. Interestingly, experts teach that when someone completely cuts off another, refusing to have anything to do with them, it's a sign of deep relational fusion. Meaning, to separate from a person fused to your emotions, you cut them off because they are too close to your trigger points.[4] This makes sense, doesn't it? If another person exists in a purely neutral space, they won't cause much of a reaction.

The twin grandsons of Abraham and Sarah, born to their long-awaited son, Isaac, portrayed the bitter grudges that can arise between family members. Even before Jacob and Esau were born, God said of these fated twins, "The older will serve the younger" (Genesis 25:23). Esau grew up to be a man of the open country, a skilled hunter. Their father, Isaac, loved Esau, but their mother, Rebekah, loved Jacob, who preferred "to stay at home among the tents" (v. 27).

Jacob was clever, and he took advantage of Esau's weakness and hunger, trading him a meal of stew for Esau's birthright, thereby usurping Esau's firstborn status. At Rebekah's bidding, Jacob later tricked Isaac into giving him the blessing that Isaac had intended for Esau. This led to Esau holding a bitter grudge against Jacob, even to the point of plotting to kill him after their father died (27:41).

Fearing for her son's life, Rebekah sent Jacob to her relatives, and Jacob stayed away from home for twenty years. During that time, he married Rachel and Leah and acquired flocks and herds. But he also did some growing. Jacob experienced trickery and mistreatment from his uncle Laban, giving him a taste of the medicine he had earlier served to Esau. He also had a life-changing encounter with God. God appeared to Jacob and reaffirmed his promises to Abraham through Jacob's line. These promises included the land of Canaan and a great number of descendants who would become a blessing for all peoples (28:13–15).

Growing discontent with Laban, Jacob set out for home with his family and animals. He was unsure of the welcome he would receive from his brother, and he prayed to God for help. He also sent a rich gift of livestock ahead in the hope of assuaging Esau's anger (32:9–18).

Finally, the day of the reunion arrived. Jacob arranged his servants, children, and flocks in groups. He went ahead, bowing down seven times as he approached his brother, Esau. Would Esau still want to kill him?

Instead, Esau ran to Jacob, threw his arms around him, and kissed him. After twenty years of separation, the twins were reunited. Jacob said to Esau, "To see your face is like seeing the face of God, now that you have received me favorably" (33:10).

There's an oft-repeated saying that "time heals all wounds." That's not quite true, of course. The rift between Jacob and Esau wasn't healed by time alone, but by personal growth and humility.

The Bible doesn't tell us what those twenty years were like for Esau. We can only imagine what experiences he had as he grew. Surely he went through trials and hardships as well as joys and successes. For Jacob's part, the hard years—paired with God's ongoing faithfulness and promises to sustain him—changed him from impertinent trickster to penitent brother. This change of character opened the door for restoration and reconciliation.

You can probably think of family members or friends whose relationships have gone sour. I know of brothers who have not spoken to each other in years and won't even speak *about* each other. It's a bit like the Pixar movie *Encanto,*[5] where the family members all agree, "We don't talk about Bruno." God's Word invites us to take an audit of our own relationships. Are there people you have wronged or held grudges against? This may not take the form of complete cutoff; sometimes it looks like harboring ill thoughts or resentment toward someone close to you without even letting them know. Do you hold on to these resentments and nurture hidden bitterness?

God wants more for you. Christ came to bring abundant life (John 10:10). This includes healed relationships. Healing and change take time—for Jacob and Esau, reconciliation took twenty long years. Hopefully it won't be quite so long for you. As it was for Jacob, healing will involve some humility. It will mean letting go of ego and pride to sincerely apologize for anything you've done wrong. This will hurt, but like Eustace letting Aslan scrape off his dragon scales in *The Voyage of the Dawn Treader*, peeling away the "old self"[6] by God's grace will open the path to true transformation and restored relationships.

Who do you need to forgive or be reconciled with? Start close: family. Even if you're not separated like Jacob and Esau, are there unresolved issues you need to work through? Come with humility. Paul wrote that God has given us a ministry of reconciliation (2 Corinthians 5:19). Forgiveness toward one another should be as complete as Christ's forgiveness for us (Colossians 3:13).

This is a picture of God restoring the world to him through the reconciling work of Christ at the cross. When we are reconciled to one another, we continue to work out the effects of Christ's redemption in our lives. Our moments of reconciliation serve as signposts pointing others to the all-encompassing work of Christ.

Who do you
need to forgive
or be reconciled
with? Start
close: family.

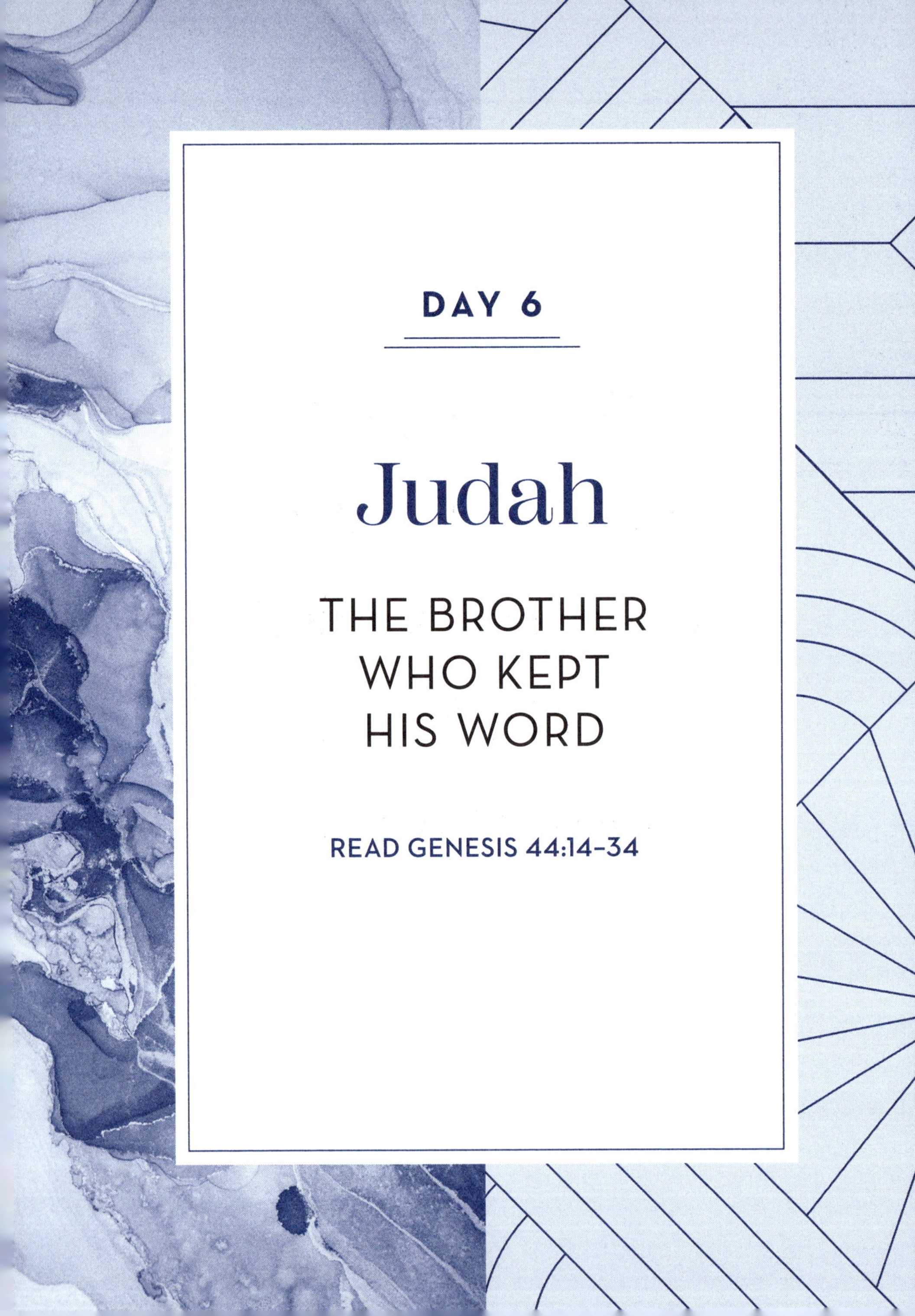

DAY 6

Judah

THE BROTHER WHO KEPT HIS WORD

READ GENESIS 44:14–34

Yesterday we reflected on the high-stakes reunion between two brothers, Jacob and Esau. Through humility, forgiveness, and God's transformation, what could have been a fight was instead a gracious reconciliation.

However, the stakes of that reunion in some ways pale in comparison to today's story. Jacob eventually had twelve sons. The two he loved the most were Joseph and Benjamin, the sons of his beloved Rachel.

In several accounts in Scripture, the leader of the other ten brothers seems to be Judah (Genesis 37:26). Although he was the fourth son in the birth order, his three older brothers (Reuben, Simeon, and Levi) had all lost their father's favor, leaving Judah with the effective status of the firstborn. Envy and jealousy of Joseph's special treatment by their father, Jacob, led the ten older brothers to sell Joseph into slavery. They covered up this treacherous act by deceiving their father into believing a wild animal had killed Joseph.

God's providence led to Joseph going from slave to prisoner to royal official in Egypt. He became second-in-command over that mighty kingdom, and he was tasked with overseeing the storing and distribution of food in the midst of a punishing famine. The famine was so severe that faraway Jacob sent his ten oldest sons, led by Judah, to Egypt to buy food. Though Joseph recognized his brothers, they didn't recognize him. Accusing them of being spies, Joseph kept his brother Simeon behind as prisoner and sent the other nine home with strict instructions not to return without their youngest brother, Benjamin. For a second time, the brothers returned to Jacob one brother short.

As the famine continued and the food ran out, Jacob told his sons to return for more. They responded that they could not go back to Egypt without Benjamin, but Jacob couldn't stand the thought of losing his youngest son. Finally Judah made a promise to his father: "I myself will guarantee his safety; you can hold me personally responsible for him. If I do not bring him back to you and set him here before you, I will bear the blame before you all my life" (Genesis 43:9). And so, Jacob let the brothers, along with Benjamin, return to Egypt.

Joseph had a test planned for his brothers to determine if they had changed. As each brother's bag was filled with food, Joseph had his own silver cup stowed in Benjamin's bag so that he could accuse Benjamin of theft when the brothers attempted to return home. Then he laid out his offer: "The man who was found to have the cup will become my slave. The rest of you, go back to your father in peace" (44:17). Twice before they had gone back to their father without a brother. Their behavior suggested they'd do the same thing again.

In a climactic and beautiful moment, Judah finally stepped up to protect one of his brothers. In an impassioned and pleading speech, Judah kept his promise to his father. He begged the still-unrecognized Joseph to take him, Judah, in Benjamin's place. He put himself on the line for his brother, out of love and loyalty to his father. Joseph finally saw that his brothers, led by Judah, had changed, and the family was restored (45:1–15).

There is a rich biblical theme of people laying their lives on the line for others. Moses laid himself on the line for the Israelites (Exodus 32:32). Esther put herself on the line to save her people (Esther 4:16). But most importantly, Jesus Christ laid down his life to save sinners. In this way, Judah's act of loyalty in offering to lay down his life for Benjamin is a powerful foreshadowing of the work of Jesus Christ, who was a descendant of the tribe of Judah.

We live in an observably selfish age. People want to accumulate toys

Sacrificing out
of love for God
means going
against culture.

and glory for themselves. They want to gain influence and followers. Sacrificing out of love for God means going against culture. Instead of feeding our egos, we are to pour ourselves out as a living sacrifice to God (Romans 12:1–3). It doesn't necessarily mean that our lives need to be put at physical risk. Instead, it means living out Paul's call in Philippians 2:5–11 to have the same mindset as Christ, who emptied himself for the sake of others so that every tongue might confess that "Jesus Christ is Lord" (v. 11). This can take the form of acts of service, spending time with people who need support, and putting the needs of others above your own interests.

It won't take long for you to think of ways to do this in your daily life. Pray that God will open your eyes for the right opportunities. It doesn't need to be dramatic—little acts of selfless love are signposts of the kingdom of heaven, and God is inviting you to pepper your own life with them now.

DAY 7

Joseph

THE MAN WHO SAW THROUGH GOD'S EYES

READ GENESIS 50:15–21

True forgiveness is among the hardest things a person can offer. It involves letting go of a wrong that another person has done to you. Even our own family members can treat us in ways that seem utterly unforgivable—and without the transforming grace of God, that is likely the case. However, when we see through God's eyes instead of our own, forgiveness is possible. Joseph showed us what that looks like.

We barely scratched the surface yesterday of how Joseph's older brothers treated him terribly. Sure, Joseph could have been a little more tactful about sharing his dreams with them—dreams in which they all bowed down to him—and a little more cautious about flaunting the special robe their father, Jacob, had given him. The brothers' response, however, was over the top. They threw Joseph into a well, planning to kill him. They even ignored the sound of their brother's cries for help (Genesis 42:21). Fortunately, a caravan of merchants passed by while Joseph was in the well, and his brothers decided to sell him rather than kill him. Though the brothers chose to spare Joseph's life, selling their brother as a slave was clearly a cruel act.

The merchants took Joseph to Egypt, where he became a slave in a high-ranking official's household. At first he ascended in status; the official, Potiphar, favored Joseph and entrusted him with the care of his household. However, a false accusation from Potiphar's wife resulted in Joseph being thrown into prison.

But God was with Joseph all along, even in prison (39:21). A providential series of actions led to Joseph becoming the second most powerful official in Egypt, subject only to the pharaoh himself.

In the last reflection, we examined the powerful reunion between Joseph and his brothers in which Judah's act of loyalty and faithfulness brought the family back together. Jacob lived out the rest of his years in Egypt. Fittingly, he lived seventeen years after he was reunited with Joseph; Joseph had been seventeen years old when his brothers sold him.

After Jacob's death, however, Joseph's older brothers grew afraid. They wondered if he had indeed forgiven them, or if his kindness had only been an act while their father was still alive. With Jacob dead, the brothers feared Joseph would finally exact his revenge upon them for their treachery to him. They sent Joseph a message that their father's final wish was for Joseph to forgive them, and then they came to Joseph and bowed down before him.

Far from feeling vindicated or haughty, Joseph felt brokenhearted. Did they really think he still harbored vengeance in his heart? Certainly, through human eyes, that would have been understandable. But Joseph didn't see his situation and struggles from his own perspective. Instead, he saw the whole story from a God's-eye view. In one of the most powerful statements on God's providence in the entire Bible, Joseph said to his brothers, "You intended to harm me, but God intended it for good" (50:20).

Romans 8:28 assures us that "in all things God works for the good of those who love him." It's not easy for us to understand how this works. Sometimes, like Joseph, it is only after many years that we can see how God's hand was at work all along.

It's also true, though, that in some cases we simply don't see God's grand plan, at least not on this side of eternity. Such times give us opportunities to practice faith in God. His plan is beyond what our eyes can see. For our part, we can try to be like Joseph. Instead of viewing life only in terms of how good or bad it's been to us, we can look for the broader design of God. We, too, should strive to see life—even through the difficult seasons—from a God's-eye view.

We should strive
to see life—
even through
the difficult
seasons—from a
God's-eye view.

The Sierpinski triangle is an interesting image. In this wonderful mathematical pattern, a person can choose any starting point within an equilateral triangle and proceed to bisect imaginary lines to any of the triangle's angles.[7] Though each angle and line is random, if you put a dot at the bisected point of each line segment, a beautiful pattern emerges. It's an incredible illustration of God's providence: Even when life seems random and chaotic, nothing happens outside of God's providential design. The more we remember and believe this, the more we echo the amazing faithfulness of Joseph.

DAY 8

Shiphrah and Puah

WOMEN WHO PROTECTED THE VULNERABLE

READ EXODUS 1:15–21

One of the classic questions of ethics is, When is it okay to break a rule to achieve a greater good? For example, is it ever okay to take what isn't yours to help a starving person? Or, as in our story today, is it okay to lie to protect human life? When asked what the greatest commandment was, Jesus offered a twofold answer: love of God and love of neighbor (Mark 12:28–34). These commands, taken from Deuteronomy and Leviticus, are to be the guiding principle of all our behavior.

Shiphrah and Puah were remarkable women. When the pharaoh of Egypt grew fearful of the power of the growing population of Israelites in his country, he subjected them to forced labor. Made into a slave class, the Israelites were compelled to build storage cities and building projects for Egypt, all while harsh taskmasters worked them ruthlessly. However, this act of enslaving the people he feared was not enough for the king.

In a command that foreshadowed Herod's attempt to kill the baby Jesus (Matthew 2:16), the pharaoh commanded the midwives who assisted in Hebrew deliveries to kill any baby boys born to the Hebrew women. Shiphrah and Puah, however, feared God, not Pharaoh (Exodus 1:16–17).

Shiphrah and Puah disobeyed the pharaoh's command in a bold act of faithfulness to God. Rather than fearing for their own lives, they courageously protected the lives of others. When the pharaoh summoned them to give an account of why the baby boys were not being killed as he commanded, they lied, saying they simply weren't able to make it to the birth in time to obey him. Far from condemning the midwives' deceit, God rewarded them for fearing and obeying him rather than the king of Egypt (1:20–21).

As we remember the faithfulness of these heroic Hebrew midwives, our goal should not be to find places in our lives where it is okay to lie. These amazing women teach us a much greater lesson. In the face of powerful voices or authorities around us, we need to remember that our highest allegiance is to God. Like Jesus said, we need to fear and honor God over humans (Matthew 10:28).

Thankfully, most of us do not live in contexts where our lives are under the same perilous threat as the Israelites in Egypt. Nonetheless, there are still believers in many parts of the world who risk comfort, status, or even their lives for their obedience to God.

The story of Shiphrah and Puah reminds us that our focus should always be fixed on faithful obedience to God. These two women stood up against the most powerful man in their world and stood firm in faithfulness to God, a wonderful testimony that our strength is not in ourselves, not in our power or status or human resources. Our strength is in God alone, who invites us to be his faithful witnesses today, just like Shiphrah and Puah were faithful witnesses so many centuries ago.

In the face of powerful voices or authorities around us, we need to remember that our highest allegiance is to God.

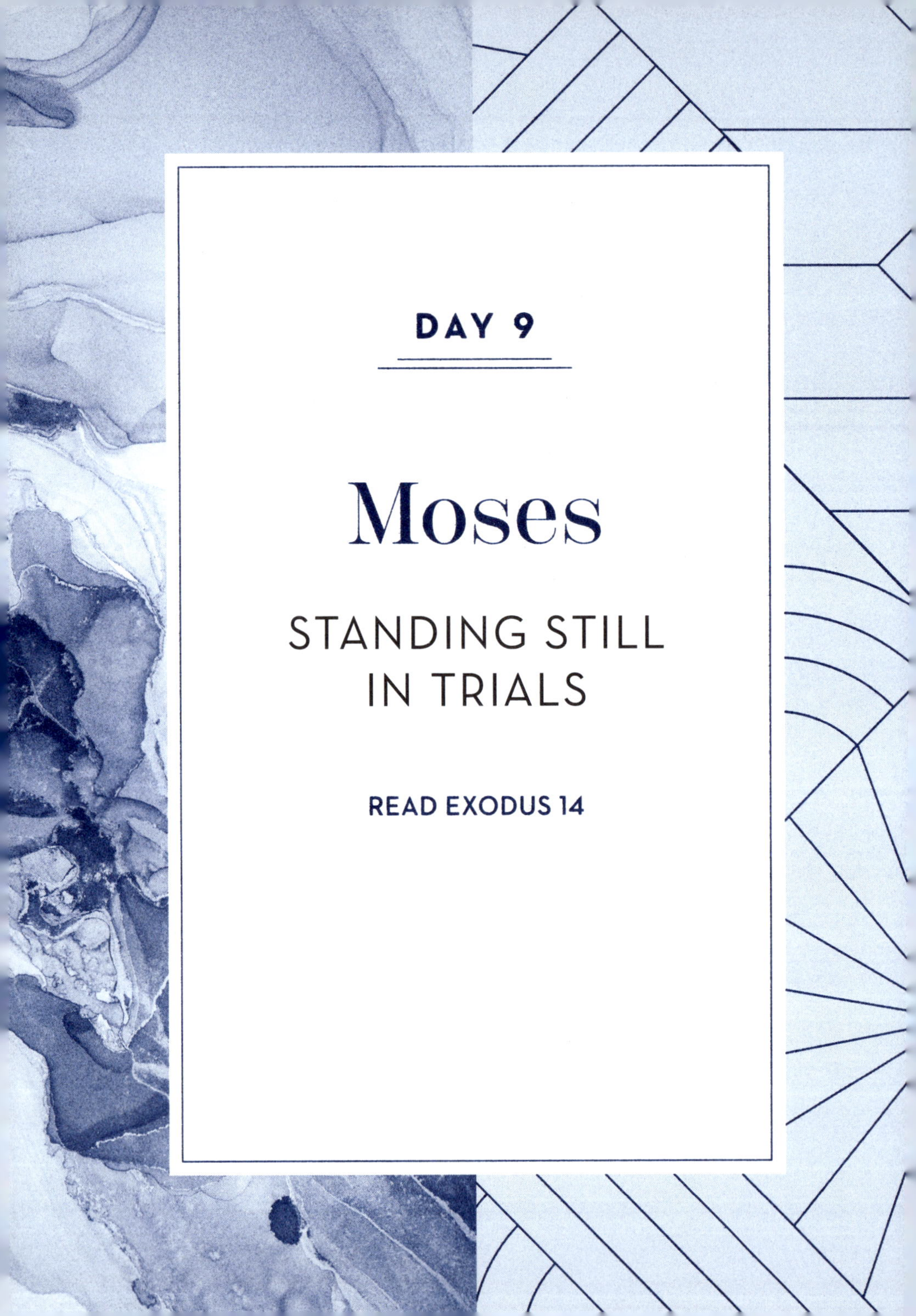

DAY 9

Moses

STANDING STILL IN TRIALS

READ EXODUS 14

Moments of desperation or anxiety can bring out the worst in us if we aren't careful. We lash out in our own strength or abandon all hope in despair. In Exodus 14, Moses showed us another way—the faithful way—to respond in moments of deep stress. We can stand firm in God and listen to his voice.

Though born a slave, Moses grew up in the privileged setting of Pharaoh's household. He presumably lived comfortably in that setting. But God planted a hunger for justice in Moses. Seeing his fellow Israelites mistreated by harsh Egyptian slave masters, Moses took matters into his own hands. He attacked and killed one of the Egyptians to protect a Hebrew slave. When his crime was found out, Moses fled to Midian.

In Midian Moses lived as a shepherd, caring for his father-in-law's flocks. He probably thought he would live out his days in peace. After forty years, however, God called him to return to Egypt to confront Pharaoh. Though Moses resisted, God was adamant: Moses was his chosen servant to free the Israelites from their slavery.

God delivered the Israelites in a dramatic way, with a series of plagues that put the false gods of Egypt to shame. Through all this, Moses (and everyone else!) witnessed the mighty power of God firsthand. Yet the conflict with Egypt wasn't finished. God led Israel and Egypt to one final dramatic showdown at the edge of the Red Sea.

As they reached an immovable sea, the Israelites began to panic when they saw their enemies approaching, and they cried out in anger toward Moses for leading them out of Egypt (Exodus 14:11–12). Moses, however, knew by now to trust in God's power, no matter how dire the situation looked. He told the people, "Do not be afraid. Stand firm and you will see the deliverance the Lord will bring you today. The

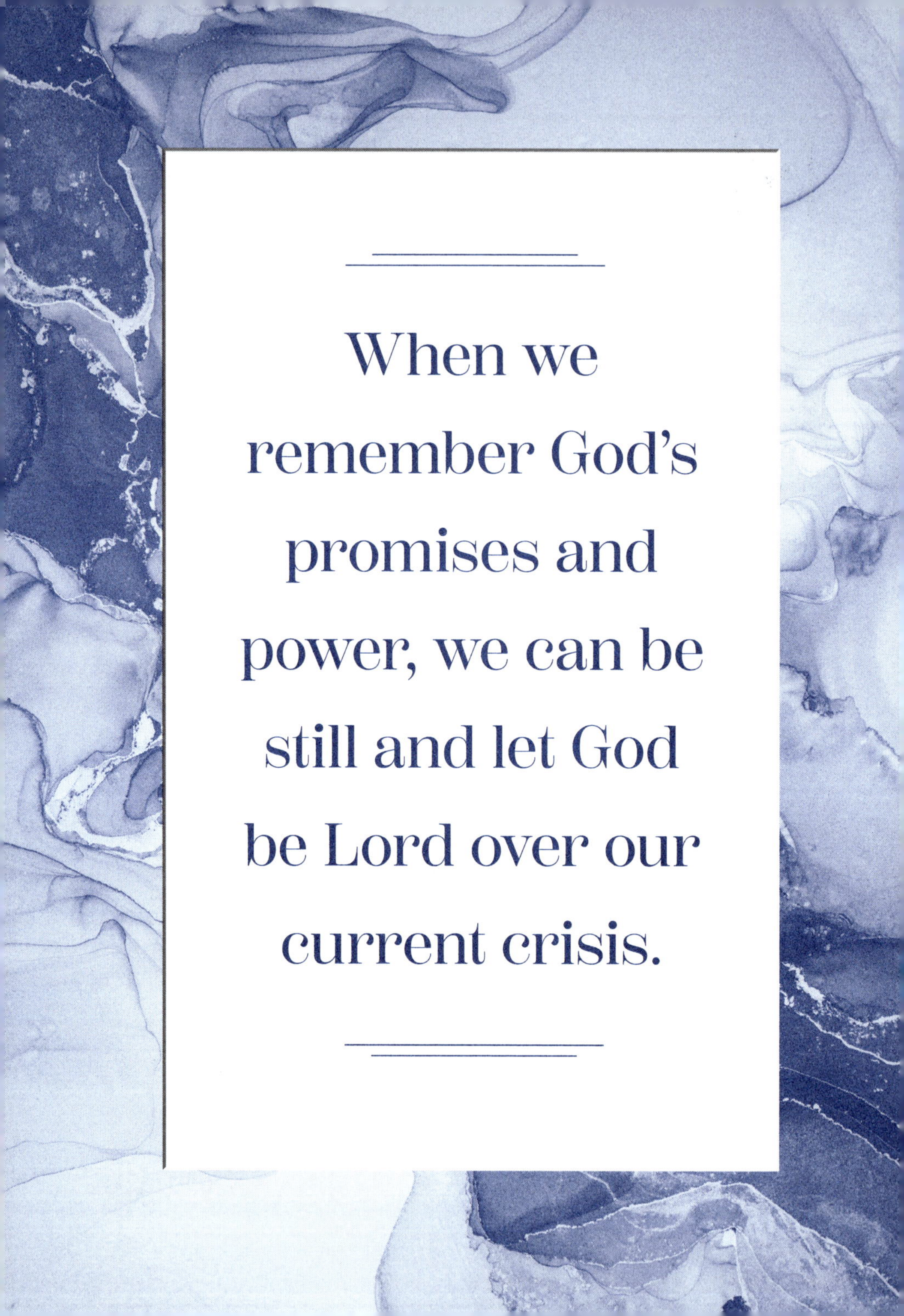
When we remember God's promises and power, we can be still and let God be Lord over our current crisis.

Egyptians you see today you will never see again. The LORD will fight for you; you need only to be still" (vv. 13–14). What an amazing promise!

God did indeed fight for his people that day. He told Moses to raise his staff over the waters, which parted before the people and allowed them to cross on dry ground. God then moved his presence from in front of the people to behind, protecting them from their enemies. And in a final act of liberation from their enslavers, God wiped out the Egyptian army in the presence of the Israelites.

Psalm 46 describes God's voice ringing clear over the chaos and battles of the world: "Be still, and know that I am God; I will be exalted among the nations, I will be exalted in the earth" (v. 10). This verse echoes what Israel witnessed when everything looked hopeless. The Lord fought for them; they only needed to be still.

Every person will have a point in life where they feel trapped, like the Israelites. Perhaps it's from extreme pressure at work, conflict with family, the heavy toll of mental health issues, or a struggle with addiction. Like the Israelites, we might be tempted to despair, not seeing any way out of a predicament. Yet God gives us grace and strength. When we remember God's promises and power, we can be still and let God be Lord over our current crisis.

The testimony of Moses is also a reminder that faithfulness is not only about our individual spiritual gain. Moses spoke God's power and promises when others were panicking. Who do you know who feels trapped and consumed by despair? Consider how God might be calling you to be his voice of comfort and joy in their lives, pointing them to the Rock that is higher than all our worries or storms (Psalm 61:2).

When you feel desperate and fearful, lashing out won't help. Neither will sinking into despair. God is your help. When you feel trapped and hopeless, be still and remember that God is your ever-present help in trouble. By God's grace and Spirit, you'll receive the strength you need to face the moment before you. God may not deliver you from every storm, but he is certainly in every storm with you, sustaining you by his loving strength.

DAY 10

Zelophehad's Daughters

SISTERS SEEKING JUSTICE

READ NUMBERS 27:1–11

After fleeing Egypt, Moses led the Israelite people into the desert, where God began to establish the law and customs that would set his people apart as unique among the nations. God brought them to the edge of the land he had promised long ago to Abraham's descendants. But when ten of the twelve spies sent to scout Canaan reported giant enemies, the generation who followed Moses out of Egypt refused to enter. God responded to their lack of faith and rebellion by allowing them to wander in the wilderness for forty years.

After forty years, God's people prepared to enter the promised land. But the five daughters of Zelophehad had a problem. The land allotments were apportioned to the men in each family. Zelophehad, who had died during the Israelites' wilderness wanderings, left behind only daughters. In an act of boldness, these daughters stood up for their cause, approaching Moses and "the whole assembly at the entrance to the tent of meeting" (Numbers 27:2). They reasoned, "Why should our father's name disappear from his clan because he had no son? Give us property among our father's relatives" (v. 4).

Moses brought the case before God and received a remarkable reply from the Lord: "What Zelophehad's daughters are saying is right. You must certainly give them property as an inheritance among their father's relatives and give their father's inheritance to them" (v. 7). God then instructed Moses to declare a new law for all future cases like that of Zelophehad's daughters. In Joshua 17:3–4, when Joshua divided the land allotments for the tribes of Israel, Zelophehad's daughters reminded Joshua and the leaders of Israel of the Lord's command to Moses, and Joshua gave them a land inheritance along with their male relatives.

Speaking and acting for justice is a pattern throughout the Bible.

God instructs his people to show special concern for the most vulnerable in society.

In the first five books of the Old Testament, we find special concern for groups such as widows, orphans, the poor, and foreigners. The demand for justice for the marginalized and vulnerable also pervades many of the Old Testament prophets. Isaiah pleaded with God's people to turn from their hypocritical religious practice and to instead "do right; seek justice. Defend the oppressed. Take up the cause of the fatherless; plead the case of the widow" (Isaiah 1:17). Jesus shared this concern, caring for the overlooked and decrying many of the religious leaders of his day for taking advantage of the oppressed rather than helping them (Mark 12:40). God instructs his people to show special concern for the most vulnerable in society.

Taking up the cause of justice is no less important today. It's true that promoting just causes will not always make you popular, even in the church. Issues that were not even debated years ago now divide us, and even pastors have felt the brunt of the polarized culture we live in now as they deliver messages and pray over their congregations. This is a sad reality in God's church today.

The story of Zelophehad's daughters reminds us and challenges us to pursue justice in light of the gospel. It may rank among the lesser-known stories in Scripture, but it proclaims an important message that God uses unlikely and unassuming individuals for great purposes. This is a lesson worth remembering!

Like these daughters, we need to speak for the causes of justice in our communities. How can you become more involved in God's justice work around you? Are there ministries or charities you can support or volunteer for that provide care for the poor, for immigrants, for veterans, for recovering addicts, or for single mothers? Remember that central to faithfulness is how we treat and care for other people.

DAY 11

Joshua

MONUMENT MAKER

READ JOSHUA 4

Where I live in the Southwest, there are many hiking trails demarcated by cairns, piled rocks that mark a path. Hikers from years past set up these cairns to mark routes for future hikers to find their way. These cairns remind me of the story in Joshua 4, where rocks served as a guide for future generations to remember the acts of God and to walk faithfully in his path.

Even before Moses appointed Joshua as his successor (Numbers 27:18), Joshua had demonstrated his faithfulness. He was one of only two spies out of the twelve who Moses sent to survey Canaan who believed in God's power to deliver the promised land to Israel (Numbers 13). Joshua trusted God more than he feared any humans or armies. In the book of Joshua, we read how he stepped boldly and faithfully into his position as Israel's leader after Moses' death.

After forty years, Israel entered the promised land through the miraculously parted waters of the Jordan River. God instructed Joshua to tell twelve men, one from each of the tribes of Israel, to each take a stone from the dry riverbed where Israel crossed the Jordan. Joshua had these stones set up as a memorial of what God had done for Israel. He told the people that these stones were to serve as visual aids for God's power in the future. When their children in years to come asked what the twelve stones meant, the Israelites were to use that opportunity to tell their children what God had done.

The stone memorial Joshua set up for the Israelites demonstrated the importance of remembering. Like hikers setting up cairns and the Israelites setting up memorial stones, we, too, should tell and retell what God has done. Remembering God's goodness strengthens our faith for the future.

Perhaps you have a "memorial stone" in your family that reminds

Remembering God's goodness strengthens our faith for the future.

you of who you are and what God has brought you through, such as a table where your family gathered for dinner and prayers or a folded flag to memorialize a former soldier who was a strong leader in the Christian faith. What are the objects and reminders in your life that tell of God's faithfulness and love to you? What "memorials" cause you to pause and reflect on God's goodness? Having reminders prompts us to reflect on God's faithfulness and strengthens our faithful response to him. They also create opportunities to tell others of God's grace so that we can pass on stories of God's works to the next generation.

DAY 12

Rahab

THE PROSTITUTE WHO PROFESSED

READ JOSHUA 2

The sins of the Canaanites were so extreme that God intended to wipe them out. And Rahab, a Canaanite prostitute, would be an unlikely candidate to become a hero of faith.

Yet when Joshua sent two spies to scope out Jericho before the Israelites entered Canaan, Rahab showed herself to be a woman of amazing faith and courage. The spies, hoping to evade capture, stayed in Rahab's house. When the king of Jericho demanded that Rahab hand them over, she lied to the king. She hid the spies and told the king's men the Israelites had already fled the city. She put herself on the line to save these strangers.

Rahab showed her amazing faith in God when she spoke to the Israelite spies: "The Lord your God is God in heaven above and on the earth below" (Joshua 2:11). What a remarkable profession! How could Rahab have such a strong faith in the God of Israel? The answer can only be that God's Spirit ignited this faith within her, and to her credit, she lived out this faith boldly.

Rahab did make a request of the spies: that she and her family would be saved when Israel conquered Jericho. The men made her a conditional promise: If she hung a scarlet cord from her window, everyone in her house would be saved on the day of battle. Rahab—a Canaanite prostitute—became a part of the covenant promise. She saved not only the Israelite spies but also her own family.

Rahab is highly honored later in the New Testament. Hebrews 11:31 lists her among the heroes of faith. James 2:25 says she was "considered righteous" for her faithful act. The highest honor of all, however, comes in Matthew 1:5, where Rahab is listed in the royal bloodline of Jesus Christ.

May Rahab's story encourage us not to make quick judgments about others. It is easy for us to see what someone looks like or hear what

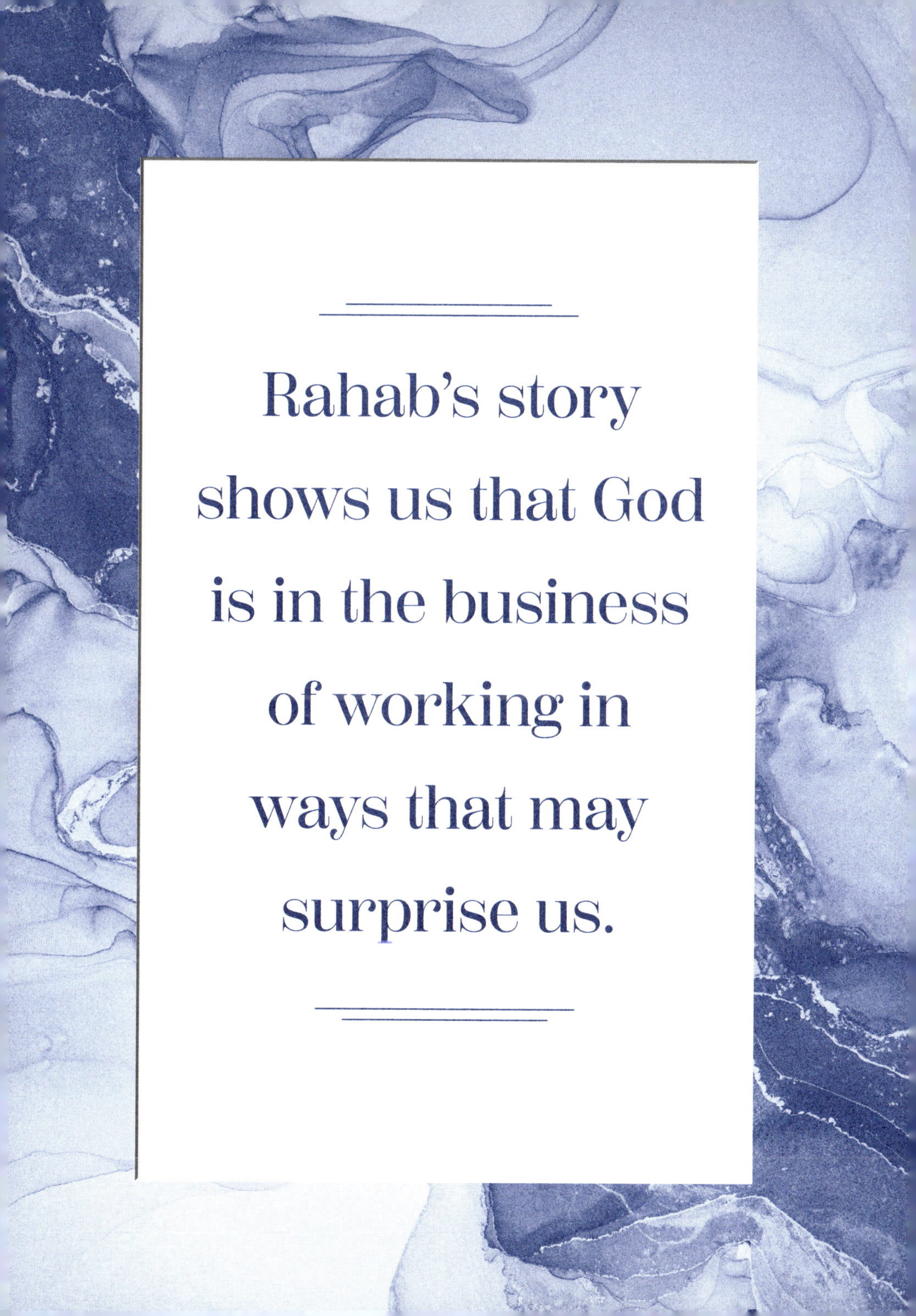
Rahab's story shows us that God is in the business of working in ways that may surprise us.

they've done in the past and stereotype them negatively. We rarely look for God to do remarkable things. Our imaginations are too small. Rahab's story reminds us to avoid judging where the lines of God's mercy fall. Like so many interactions in Christ's ministry, Rahab's story shows us that God is in the business of working in ways that may surprise us.

Perhaps you feel more like Rahab in this story, unworthy or not good enough because of mistakes you've made. Maybe you carry guilt about things you've done. Let Rahab's story offer comfort and inspiration: God doesn't judge people by worldly résumés or outward appearances. He looks at the heart (1 Samuel 16:7). Your past mistakes do not keep you from a life of faithfulness. You can be part of God's work. It's his power that you rely on, not your own. God includes all kinds of people in his redemption story.

Gideon

THE COWARD WHO BECAME A LEADER

READ JUDGES 7

When the film director Steven Spielberg showed his film *Schindler's List* to composer John Williams, Williams was so taken by the power of the movie that he told Spielberg he would need a better composer for the film's score. Spielberg responded to Williams by saying, "But they're all dead"—no better composer was available![8]

Sometimes a task falls upon your shoulders, and even though you don't feel equipped, you're the one called to do it. Such was the case with Gideon. Gideon was one of the judges God selected to lead his people as they fought enemies in the land of Canaan. God commissioned Gideon to lead Israel in a fight against their powerful enemies, the Midianites.

However, at the beginning, Gideon looked like anything but leadership material. His story began during a time when the Midianites were terrorizing the people of Israel, destroying crops and killing livestock. Gideon was first introduced threshing wheat in a winepress. Since that may not mean anything to you, let me offer some context. Threshing wheat usually involved tossing it into the air so a breeze could blow away the lighter chaff, leaving the heavier grain behind. Which means a winepress, basically a pit, was a terrible place for the task—there is no crosswind down in a hole.

Gideon was not in the winepress because he was a terrible farmer. He was there because he was afraid of his enemies. It was this moment, with Gideon looking utterly weak and fearful, that God's angel appeared before him, saying, "The Lord is with you, mighty warrior" (Judges 6:12). Things certainly didn't look that way!

Gideon's journey from the winepress to faithful leadership was a process, one of slowly learning to see the world through God's eyes rather than through his own doubts. At first Gideon resisted, but in the end God's call upon his life prevailed. God was patient with Gideon's faulty faith.

When the time came for Gideon to lead the fight against the Midianites, God didn't make things easy. He told Gideon to send home any soldiers who were afraid of battle, and twenty-two thousand soldiers left the army. (It's not hard to imagine Gideon wishing he was one of them!) But God told Gideon his army was still too large. God wanted to leave no doubt that Israel's victory was due to God's own miraculous power. After God pared down the size of Israel's army a second time, Gideon was left with only three hundred soldiers. That was a paltry contingent compared to the hordes of their enemies.

On the eve of battle, Gideon was afraid. God encouraged him by letting him overhear a Midianite soldier tell another about a dream he had in which Gideon defeated them. Finally emboldened, Gideon armed his men for war—but not with weapons. Rather, he gave them each a trumpet and a torch hidden under a clay pot. The three hundred men surrounded the enemy camp while it was still dark, and at Gideon's signal they smashed the pots to let the light from their torches shine brightly. They blew their trumpets and shouted, "A sword for the LORD and for Gideon!" (7:20). God caused the terrified Midianites to turn on one another with their swords. Israel gained a victory with only three hundred men, shining torches, and loud trumpets.

There will be times when God asks us to trust him in the face of uncertain or unlikely circumstances. Like Gideon, our first inclination might be doubt, fear, and resistance. Yet, again and again in the Bible, God is patient with these human reactions. Gideon's story is a reminder that we cannot always trust our own eyes or assumptions. God may surprise us, using very little for great purposes.

Sometimes you may feel you are not qualified for a task or a position. The reality is, there are no "super" Christians. Everyone is on an imperfect journey of following Christ. Christ himself reminds us that even a mustard seed of faith is enough to move mountains in God's kingdom (Matthew 17:20). As Gideon's army learned, it's not our own qualifications but God's power that makes a difference.

What makes you feel doubt or fear in your walk of faith? When do you feel like you aren't "good enough" to be used by God? Let Gideon's story be an encouragement to you. God is patient. He knows your doubts and fears. Your hope is not in what you can or can't do on your own. It is in God's faithful patience to develop you and work through you.

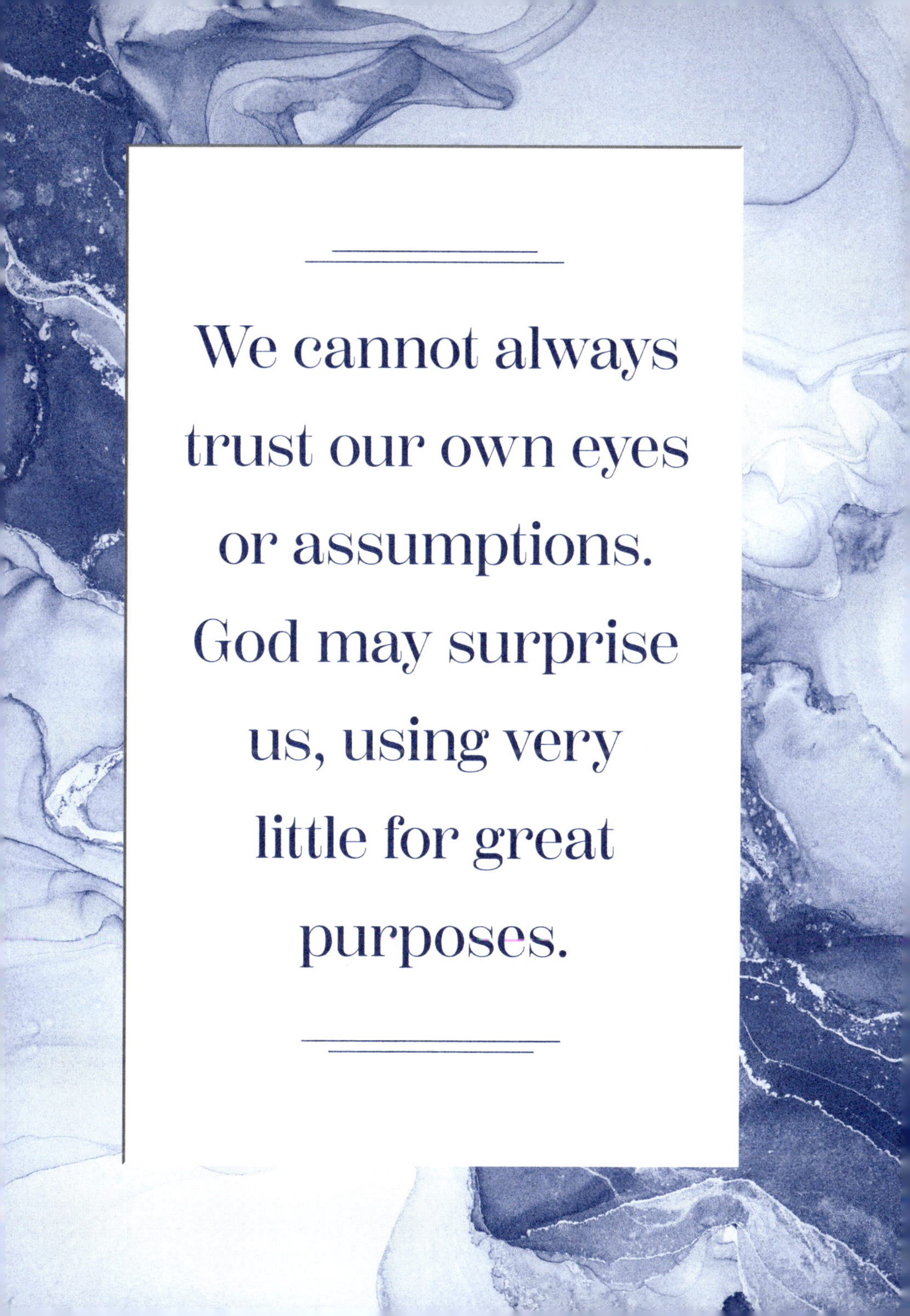
We cannot always trust our own eyes or assumptions. God may surprise us, using very little for great purposes.

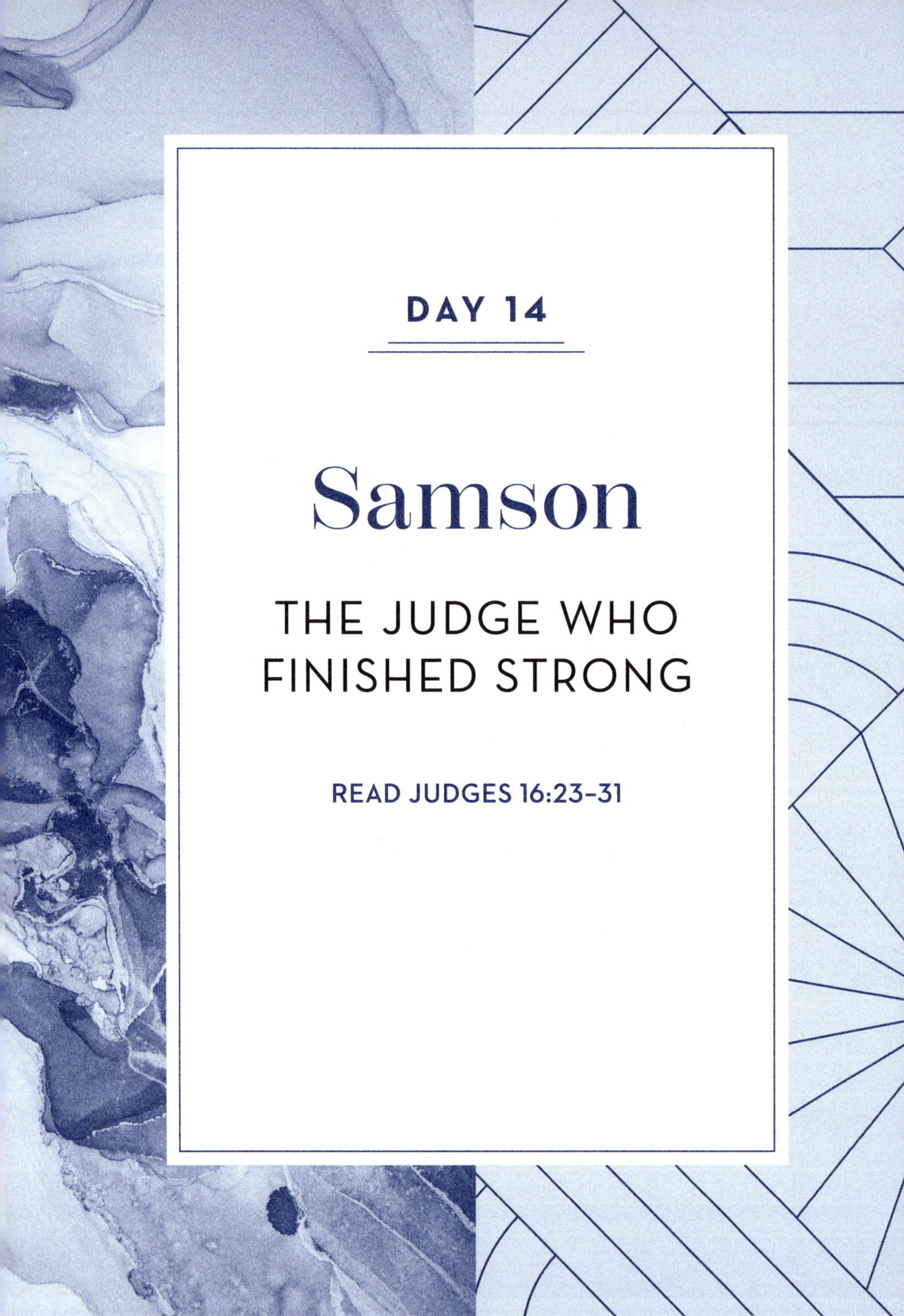

DAY 14

Samson

THE JUDGE WHO FINISHED STRONG

READ JUDGES 16:23–31

You may be surprised to see Samson in this survey of faith. Samson's life is a favorite Bible story for many: the long hair, superhuman strength, defeating of an army with nothing but a donkey's jawbone, and of course his fateful relationship with Delilah. It's all wonderful storytelling. But Samson, for most of his life, was deeply flawed. He was set apart for God's service from birth, but he didn't live a very godly life. He certainly is not presented as a man of prayer. He broke the Nazirite rules he was supposed to follow. He had a roving eye for women, and he was violent. How can his life illustrate how we can be faithful now?

Let's pause to remember something about God's providence. God can use unlikely people, even unfaithful people, to accomplish his will. As we saw in Joseph's story, God can use difficult circumstances and wicked motives to good ends. At times God used Israel's enemies—sometimes to punish them, sometimes to liberate them (as in the case of Cyrus of Persia in 2 Chronicles 36:22–23). In the same way, God used Samson, messy though he was. The Israelites were under the oppressive hand of the Philistines, and God used Samson to take the lead in delivering God's people from their oppressors (Judges 13:5).

Now, this is all well and good, but what does this have to show us about faithful living in our own lives? We know God calls us to righteousness and holiness; Paul warned against the mindset of being loose on sin: "Shall we go on sinning so that grace may increase? By no means! We are those who have died to sin; how can we live in it any longer?" (Romans 6:1–2). We'd hardly want to say, "Mimic Samson and let God work through you despite your poor behavior." Ignoring sin is not the lesson to learn from Samson's life.

Instead, Samson's life illustrates that it is never too late to return to God.

Samson's life illustrates that it is never too late to return to God.

In the final moments of Samson's life, everything had been taken from him. He was imprisoned and enslaved, doing the work of an animal by grinding grain into flour. His eyes had been gouged out and his hair had been shaved. At the pagan festival to the god Dagon, the Philistines put Samson on display to mock and torment him. He was a broken shell of a man; the term "rock bottom" doesn't do justice to how low he had sunk.

Yet, in that moment, he called upon God. He prayed for strength to accomplish God's judgment upon Israel's enemies: "Sovereign LORD, remember me" (Judges 16:28). And, like he did with the thief on the cross next to Jesus (Luke 23:42–43), God answered Samson's prayer moments before his death.

> Then Samson reached toward the two central pillars on which the temple stood. Bracing himself against them, his right hand on the one and his left hand on the other, Samson said, "Let me die with the Philistines!" Then he pushed with all his might, and down came the temple on the rulers and all the people in it. Thus he killed many more when he died than while he lived. (Judges 16:29–30)

Whatever mistakes you've made, however you may have turned away from God or faith in the past, God is a loving Father, ready to receive his children back. Faith begins and ends with God's grace, and that grace is working to draw you closer to him.

You may have a prodigal story of your own. We've all had seasons where we have strayed from—or perhaps outright rejected—God and his will. Perhaps you've had a lingering sense of God's presence, but you've pushed that to the back of your mind. Maybe you've started to question, *Is it too late for me to return to God? Have I let God down too many times, and now he won't want me back?* As with the father at the return of the prodigal son (Luke 15:20), the answer is an unequivocal *no*. God's grace keeps working to bring us back. Wherever you are, it's never too late to come back to your faithful God.

DAY 15

Ruth

THE FAITHFUL FOREIGNER

READ RUTH 1:16–22

Perhaps when you were a child your parents read picture books to you before bed, or you read to your own children now. You may have favorite ones about unbreakable love, where a parent character (often a bunny, a fox, or another animal) assures their child, *I will love you, no matter what.* These simple books of unbreakable love and faithfulness are moving. What child would not want to hear that their parents love them, no matter what?

That kind of loyalty and faithfulness is put on beautiful display in the book of Ruth. Ruth was a Moabite woman, and the Israelites did not care for the Moabites (Deuteronomy 23:3). Yet she showed the most unlikely, unwavering, inspiring loyalty and love to her mother-in-law, Naomi.

Naomi's life falls apart in the first chapter of Ruth. A severe famine sent Naomi, her husband, and their sons from Israel to the land of Moab to survive. In Moab, her husband died. Her two sons married Moabite women, but then the two sons died as well. Naomi was left empty, in a foreign land with only her two foreign daughters-in-law, Orpah and Ruth. When word reached Naomi that the famine back home in Bethlehem had finally ended, Naomi set out for Israel. Her daughters-in-law set out with her, but Naomi bid them to return to their own parents and homes. Life would be hard for Moabite widows in Israel.

Orpah returned home at Naomi's bidding, but Ruth refused to leave Naomi. In a powerful speech, Ruth professed, "Where you go I will go, and where you stay I will stay. Your people will be my people and your God my God. Where you die I will die, and there I will be buried" (Ruth 1:16–17). These are words of such total commitment that I have even heard them included in wedding vows. Ruth's loyalty to Naomi knew no limits, even though she didn't know what the future would hold.

Our society needs models of loyalty and "no matter what" love, like Ruth demonstrated.

Although circumstances were grim for the two widows in Bethlehem, God provided for them. By God's providence, Ruth gleaned for grain in the fields of Boaz. Boaz, it turned out, was a relative of Naomi's deceased husband. He took on the role of the family guardian redeemer, caring for the family in the wake of a relative's passing. Although Ruth was a foreign widow, Boaz agreed to marry her in order to care for her and for Naomi.

Both Boaz and Ruth are described as having noble and upright character, and both showed stunning loyalty and love. Unfortunately, loyalty and relationship faithfulness seem to be in short supply today. People are fickle. Often we see people put themselves first, abandoning marriages when they deem the relationship inconvenient or unexciting. Our society needs models of loyalty and "no matter what" love, like Ruth demonstrated, and commitment to noble character.

Faithfulness and loyalty are not just for children's books and Bible stories. Ruth's story invites us to reflect on the most important relationships in our lives. How can we deepen and demonstrate a Ruth-like faithfulness and loyalty to those God has placed around us, starting with our families?

Consider how you can demonstrate loyalty and selflessness in the important relationships in your life. View this assignment not as an imposition on your independence, but instead as a witness to your love and a testimony of God's grace working through you. As Christ said, the world will know we are his followers through our acts of love (John 13:35). Paul instructed Christians to be devoted to one another out of love and to honor others above ourselves (Romans 12:10). This is what true loyalty looks like—something Ruth beautifully and powerfully modeled.

DAY 16

Hannah

A LONGING MOTHER

READ 1 SAMUEL 1–2

Loneliness is one of the most universal human experiences. It comes when we lack connection and close relationships, often during seasons of change like a move to a new community. Loneliness also comes when we feel misunderstood by those around us. Even with family or friends nearby, when no one understands what we're going through, it can be incredibly isolating. This is especially true during seasons of grief. Hannah experienced this kind of isolating sadness in 1 Samuel 1.

Hannah was married to Elkanah, who also had another wife named Peninnah. Peninnah's name means "pearl" or "precious stone," and she certainly thought she was a gem. After all, she was able to produce offspring for Elkanah while Hannah could not. Yet Peninnah knew Elkanah loved Hannah more. Each year when they went to worship God at Shiloh, Elkanah gave Hannah a double portion of food compared to what he gave Peninnah. Bitter with jealousy, Peninnah took to goading Hannah with harsh words until she broke down weeping and refused to eat.

Elkanah tried to comfort Hannah, and while he meant well, we can conclude that he was rather tone-deaf to her grief: "Why are you downhearted? Don't I mean more to you than ten sons?" (v. 8). Not exactly helpful!

In her loneliness and grief, Hannah went to pray. Eli the priest saw her lips moving but heard no sound, and he assumed she'd been drinking too much. Even the spiritual leader in Hannah's life was blind to her grief!

Mistreated by Peninnah, misunderstood by Elkanah, accused of drunkenness by Eli, Hannah had nowhere to turn but to God. She poured out her heart in prayer.

Like the psalms of lament, Hannah laid out her misery before God. She didn't hide the rawness of her pain. Hannah's name means "grace," and her story certainly moves from despair to grace. God granted her a son, Samuel, who went on to become one of Israel's great leaders. In joy and gratitude, Hannah burst into a second prayer, the beautiful prayer of 1 Samuel 2:1–10. This prayer proclaims God's gracious nature of looking mercifully upon the lowly and raising up the downtrodden. Hannah's prayer is a powerful statement of faith and praise, and it is echoed by Mary's song in Luke 1:46–55. Both women praised God for his loving care toward the weak and oppressed.

Hannah is an exemplar of prayer, and her two prayers are like two sides of the coin in our relationship with God. Each one of us will go through times of despair and grief. These seasons in life can leave us feeling lonely and misunderstood by those closest to us, even our own family members. Hannah showed us how to turn to God in these moments. Her prayer is a master class on how to approach God. In times of sorrow, we can be honest and open with him. We can remember to "cast all [our] anxiety on him because he cares for [us]" (1 Peter 5:7). When life is wrought with anguish, we can bring that pain to God knowing he is always ready to hear us when we pray. God honors the prayers of his children (James 5:16). We don't need to hide our grief and pain from God.

Likewise, in times of joy—like when Hannah welcomed her son—we should not forget to praise God for his amazing mercy and love. The Bible tells us that every good and perfect gift comes from God (James 1:17). Each blessing we experience is another opportunity to praise God and give testimony of his faithfulness to others.

Prayer is one of the most important faith practices for Christians.

God honors the prayers of his children (James 5:16). We don't need to hide our grief and pain from God.

When you struggle to know what to pray, let the Bible guide you. What is your prayer life like? What distractions or behaviors keep it from flourishing? In what seasons has prayer been a vibrant part of your faith? Like any relationship, communication is key to a strong relationship with God, in which we not only bring our own needs to God but also patiently and contemplatively listen for his voice. God meets us through prayer. That was true for Hannah, and it's still true for God's faithful children today.

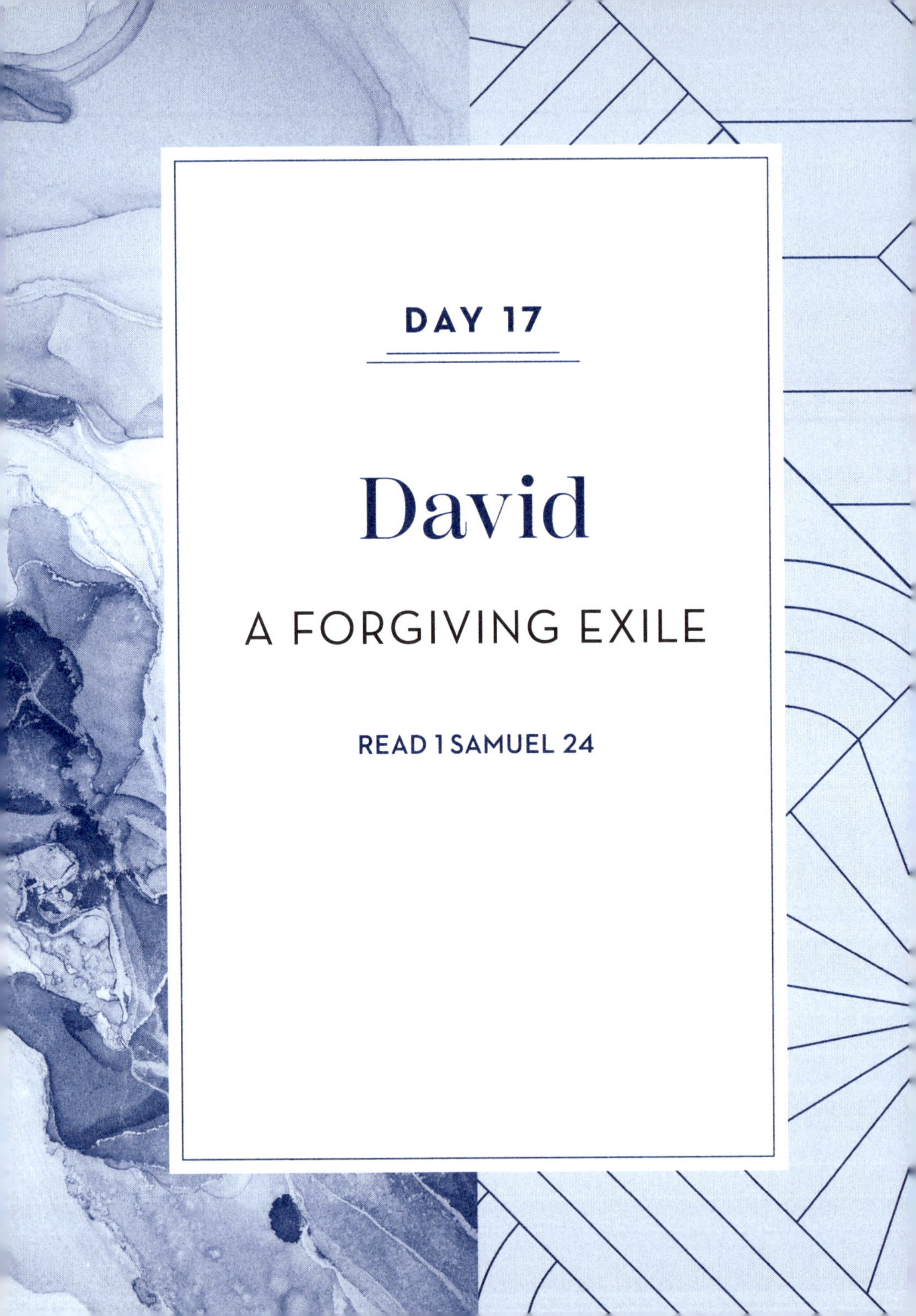

DAY 17

David

A FORGIVING EXILE

READ 1 SAMUEL 24

If you have ever been to Israel, you may have discovered one of the most memorable and beautiful places to visit is En Gedi, a valley with cool, fresh streams and lush flora in an otherwise stark and arid landscape. It is surrounded by caves, and the fresh water running through En Gedi also makes it a strategic location in an otherwise unforgiving desert.

According to 1 Samuel 24, David was hiding in En Gedi when he spared Saul's life. Saul was the first king of Israel, anointed by Hannah's son, the prophet Samuel. Initially, Saul was a successful leader, but he eventually fell out of favor with God because of his disobedience. As David, a young shepherd who served Saul as a musician and warrior, gained fame and favor among the people of Israel, Saul became increasingly jealous and paranoid.

King Saul's envy toward David led him to relentlessly pursue his future replacement, attempting to kill him again and again. Saul's hatred even turned into paranoia and violence toward those he suspected of aiding David (22:13–19). David lived on the run, traveling through the countryside with a group of men who were loyal to him. Though he was innocent of Saul's claims, he was forced to live in hiding in the wilderness.

Throughout this ordeal, however, David maintained his firm trust in God. He sought God's guidance and instruction in all he did (23:2, 4, 11). Rather than seeing his situation through the eyes of anger, fear, or despair, David relied on God.

Saul led three thousand troops (certainly a questionable use of national defense resources!) in pursuit of David into the area of En Gedi. At one point, Saul entered a cave to relieve himself, and it just so happened this was the very cave where David and his men were hiding. David's men urged him to act, insisting that God had delivered Saul into their hands, but instead of killing Saul or taking him captive, David secretly cut off a piece of the hem of Saul's robe.

After Saul left the cave, David confronted him. Affirming his own innocence and his trust in God, David said to Saul, "I have not wronged you, but you are hunting me down to take my life. May the LORD judge between you and me. And may the LORD avenge the wrongs you have done to me, but my hand will not touch you" (24:11–12).

David's words show what trusting God looks like, even when given the opportunity to take revenge. Hebrews 10:30 reminds us, "For we know him who said, 'It is mine to avenge; I will repay,' and again, 'The Lord will judge his people.'" It is a human impulse to want to take revenge into our own hands, but the Bible shows us another way. Christians should not be people set on revenge. Revenge never brings true justice. Instead, God's children are to trust God to be the just judge. Our task is not revenge; it is forgiveness. This will not always be easy, but David's faithfulness gives us a wonderful example to look to.

Vigilante justice does not bring true peace, and it betrays a lack of trust in God. He will uphold the cause of the righteous and bring justice. When we turn our hearts away from revenge and instead focus on forgiveness, we find the path of true blessing. First Peter 3:9 says, "Do not repay evil with evil or insult with insult. On the contrary, repay evil with blessing, because to this you were called so that you may inherit a blessing." Similarly, Paul instructed believers, "Make sure that nobody pays back wrong for wrong, but always strive to do what is good for each other and for everyone else" (1 Thessalonians 5:15). That's what the Christian community should look like.

When Peter asked Jesus, "Lord, how many times shall I forgive my brother or sister who sins against me? Up to seven times?" Jesus replied,

When we turn our hearts away from revenge and instead focus on forgiveness, we find the path of true blessing.

not seven, but seventy-seven (Matthew 18:21–22). This is an exaggerated number that indicates that Christ's followers should be boundlessly forgiving. David's forgiveness of Saul, who was trying relentlessly to kill him, demonstrates this kind of faithfulness and forgiveness.

Our forgiveness of others is anchored in God's forgiveness of us through Christ. Colossians 3:13 says, "Bear with each other and forgive one another if any of you has a grievance against someone. Forgive as the Lord forgave you." There is no limit to the measure of God's forgiveness for his children; all our sins are washed away. God calls us to be faithful stewards of that forgiveness in this world, extending Christlike grace to others. In echoing the faith of David by being people of radical forgiveness, we show the world the love of Christ.

Solomon

THE KING WHO SOUGHT WISDOM

READ 1 KINGS 3:4–15

A former pastor once said, "Knowledge is knowing that a tomato is a fruit, but wisdom is knowing to eat it like a vegetable. No one wants a tomato in their fruit salad!" Wisdom goes beyond knowledge. It's not just about facts; it's about living well in light of what is true.

Wisdom is a godly virtue taught throughout the Bible, and no character in the Bible is more closely associated with wisdom than King Solomon. Solomon took the throne in Jerusalem after his father, David, and led the country during a period of great prosperity.

Yet Solomon's reign models the exact opposite of what Moses hoped for Israel's future kings (Deuteronomy 17:14–20). Solomon put so much hope in his own military strength that he needed to have storage cities built just for his horses and chariots. He amassed enormous amounts of gold and wealth for himself. And he had far too many women—seven hundred wives of royal birth along with three hundred concubines. As Moses had warned, these many wives pulled Solomon's heart away from God. On top of that, Solomon subjected the people to forced labor and set taskmasters over them, sounding more like Pharaoh (Exodus 1:11–14) than like a righteous and godly king.

Yet for all of Solomon's flaws, the amazing thing is that God still helped him. Near the beginning of Solomon's reign, God appeared to him through a dream at Gibeon and offered Solomon whatever he wanted, as if handing him a blank check. Solomon responded to God by asking for wisdom: "Give your servant a discerning heart to govern your people and to distinguish between right and wrong" (1 Kings 3:9). God was pleased with Solomon and granted him wisdom beyond that of any other human—a wisdom that became legendary and pointed others to God (10:8–9).

Solomon did not walk in God's ways over the course of his whole life. Yet God's response to Solomon teaches us what God desires for each of us: a humble heart that seeks wisdom from God. And Solomon's story also demonstrates that this is something God will graciously grant to his children. Like James 1:5 says, "If any of you lacks wisdom, you should ask God, who gives generously to all without finding fault, and it will be given to you."

True wisdom comes through learning from God's Word and being attentive to God's Spirit. There are plenty of clever or knowledgeable people in the world, but real wisdom is demonstrated by living a devoted and faithful life for God.

We need wisdom in all areas of our lives. Wisdom is not simply an accessory for the Christian life; it is necessary for living well and glorifying God in all we do. It takes wisdom

- to navigate our relationships, whether with family members, friends, coworkers, or neighbors. Conflicts that come up in our lives require wisdom to resolve.
- to discern the kind of media and information we consume and believe. We all know that spending mindless time on our mobile devices or getting sucked into toxic news broadcasts is not a God-glorifying way to live, but it takes wisdom to walk a better path.
- to cut through the noise and to speak about important issues intelligently. In Jesus' disputes with the religious leaders of his day, he never stooped to the level of their squabbles or fell into their traps. He spoke wisely, even under pressure.

Real wisdom is demonstrated by living a devoted and faithful life for God.

Paul wrote in 1 Corinthians 1:24 that Christ is "the wisdom of God." Humans will always falter in walking the path of wisdom, but Christ fully embodies God's wisdom and invites us to come and learn from him. As Paul wrote, this wisdom might look like "foolishness" (v. 25) to the world around us. After all, why would Christians devote themselves to a Savior who died a criminal's death?

What seems strange to the world, however, is the very center of the good news for God's children. It is through the self-giving death and death-defeating resurrection of Christ that we find true life and hope. God opens the path of wisdom to us—a life that follows the call of Christ with a humble faithfulness that puts God on display.

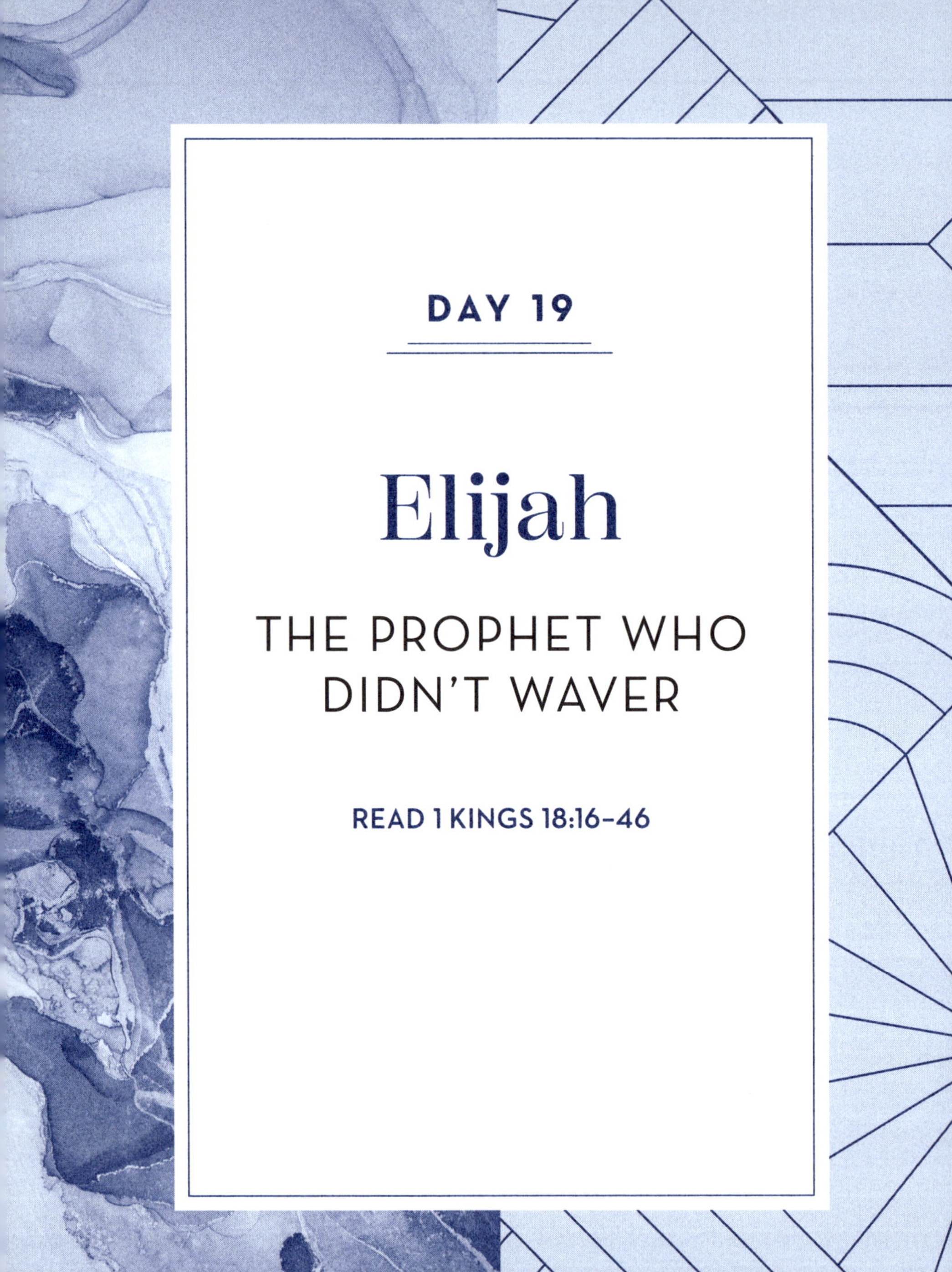

DAY 19

Elijah

THE PROPHET WHO DIDN'T WAVER

READ 1 KINGS 18:16–46

In the play and movie *Twelve Angry Men*,[9] a jury debates a court case against a nineteen-year-old boy. If the teenager is found guilty, he'll go to the electric chair. The jury's decision needs to be unanimous. All the jurors find the boy guilty . . . except for juror number 8. Juror 8 stands firmly on his own, not swayed by the majority. He is simply not convinced of the boy's guilt, and the more they discuss and reflect on the case, the more the other jurors side with juror number 8. In the end, the innocent teenager's life is saved because one juror stood firm in his convictions rather than going with the crowd.

Few characters provide as clear an example of standing alone against the crowd as Elijah facing off against the prophets of Baal and Asherah. After the reign of King Solomon, Israel split into two kingdoms: the Northern Kingdom of Israel and the Southern Kingdom of Judah. Elijah was a prophet of God who announced a famine in the land of Israel due to King Ahab's sin. Rather than repenting of his sin, Ahab blamed Elijah for the famine. In the third year of the famine, God sent Elijah, who had been living outside Israel in the area of Tyre and Sidon, to confront Ahab.

Elijah challenged Ahab to a contest: Elijah versus 450 of Ahab's pagan prophets, to call on their competing gods to see who would answer by lighting an offered bull on fire.

The odds seemed to be stacked against Elijah in this epic showdown. It was not just the issue of one prophet against hundreds. The nature of the challenge, to see which god would answer with fire from the sky, seemed to favor Baal. Ancient iconography pictures Baal with a lightning bolt in his hand, similar to the Greek god Zeus—Baal was revered as the storm god. If any god were to send fire from heaven, surely it would be Baal.

The location of the contest also favored Baal. The mountain of the God of Israel was believed to be Zion, in Judah's capital of Jerusalem. Carmel, on the other hand, was considered Baal's home turf. Furthermore, Elijah let Baal's prophets pick which bull they wanted to sacrifice, allowing them to choose the best one to please their god. What's more, Elijah soaked his own sacrificial altar with water—not exactly a conducive approach to fire building.

Having every advantage, Baal's prophets set to invoking their god to show his power. They danced and called, becoming more and more frenzied as time went on, even cutting their bodies to win their god's attention—to no avail.

The showdown between the God of Israel and Baal had an audience. Speaking to the crowds, Elijah challenged them to stop wavering between two positions: "How long will you waver between two opinions? If the LORD is God, follow him; but if Baal is God, follow him" (1 Kings 18:21). The people, hedging their bets rather than risking commitment, remained silent.

That is, until the power of God was unleashed before their eyes. At the time of the evening sacrifice, Elijah called on God to send fire from heaven, "so these people will know that you, LORD, are God, and that you are turning their hearts back again" (v. 37). Fire poured down from heaven, consuming the sacrifice, the altar, and the water that had soaked it all. The people finally responded with a declaration of faith: "The LORD—he is God!" (v. 39).

Elijah demonstrated the power in standing firm for God, even when it meant standing alone. When we know God's love and God's will, no amount of peer pressure can sway us from our convictions. We don't need to be afraid; we know God and we trust in him alone. Elijah had a

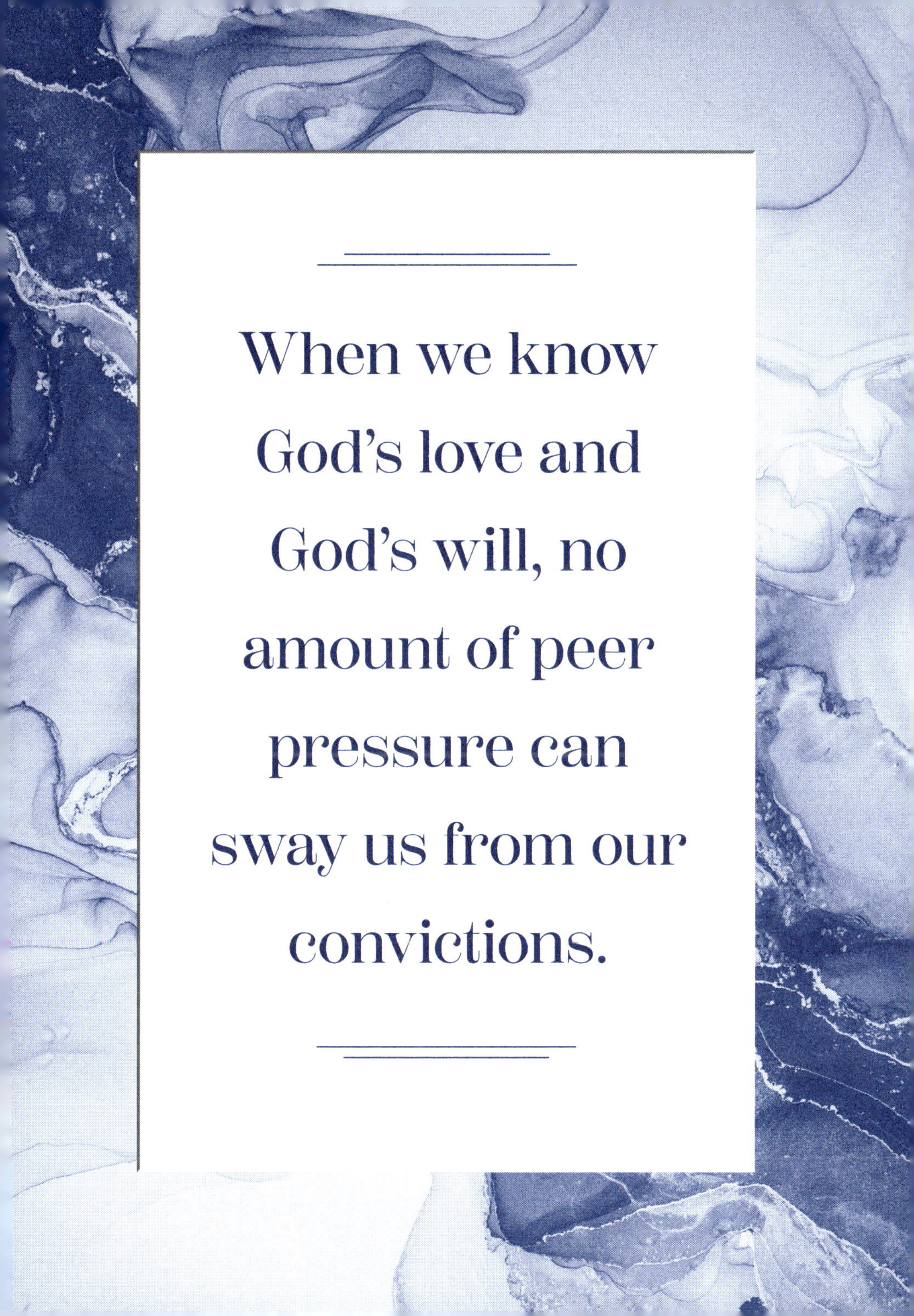
When we know God's love and God's will, no amount of peer pressure can sway us from our convictions.

real and deep relationship with God. The fact that there were hundreds of prophets of Baal on the mountain while he was the only prophet of God didn't sway him in the least. Neither should we be swayed in our faith by the voices or influences around us. What we have seen and experienced, planted within us by the gift of faith, is the life-giving message and power of Christ. Even when we stand alone, we stand faithfully in that power.

DAY 20

Naaman

ENEMY TURNED BELIEVER

READ 2 KINGS 5

Many of us struggle to wrap our minds around God's grace and feel we need to earn it somehow. We try to make things more complicated than they need to be. Grace is so simple that it can be hard for us to understand or accept. So many of us are "doers," and we think there must be more boxes to check and tests to pass. That was certainly the case for Naaman.

Naaman was an unlikely person to put his faith in the God of Israel. He was an Aramean general, an enemy of God's people who was highly regarded by the king of Aram. But Naaman had a problem: He was afflicted with leprosy.

One day, hope came from an unlikely place. A Hebrew slave girl, who had been taken from Israel by Aramean raiders, lived in Naaman's household and served his wife. We would hardly hold it against this unnamed Hebrew girl if she secretly celebrated Naaman's leprosy, seeing it as God's punishment upon him for the pain he inflicted on Israel. But instead, the young girl told Naaman's wife where she believed Naaman could go to be healed: the prophet Elisha, in Israel.

Naaman brought gifts fit for a king to give to the man who could heal his leprosy. When his impressive caravan arrived at Elisha's house, however, Elisha didn't even step outside to greet him. He sent his servant out to Naaman, giving him such simple instructions for being healed that it sounded silly. "Go, wash yourself seven times in the Jordan, and your flesh will be restored and you will be cleansed" (2 Kings 5:10).

Naaman was *not* impressed. We can certainly imagine that Naaman had tried time and again to wash himself clean, to no avail. Furthermore, Naaman considered the Jordan to be a rather uninspiring river to wash in. There were much grander rivers back in Aram. Naaman had hoped for a grand display, for a powerful miracle worker to wave his hands and

People with comfortable lives who look like they have everything they need still need God's healing presence.

say effective incantations. Seven dips in the Jordan sounded like foolishness, and Naaman almost walked away.

Fortunately, Naaman's officers convinced him to at least try what Elisha had said. It seemed too simple, but what did he have to lose? Naaman acquiesced, and his skin became as pure and clean as that of a young child (v. 14). He was transformed by the experience, professing his full devotion to the God of Israel: "Now I know that there is no God in all the world except in Israel" (v. 15). Naaman even took some dirt from Israel back home to Aram so that he could worship the God of Israel on Israelite soil regardless of where he lived.

Naaman's story shows us that even people who are powerful and wealthy, people with comfortable lives who look like they have everything they need still need God's healing presence. We can grow complacent in our comfortable homes and with our endless sources of entertainment. We need to remember that all those externals don't meet our spiritual need. Naaman's problem was visible, on his skin. Our spiritual condition, however, is invisible.

As we see with Naaman, what begins as a yearning for healing ends in an experience of grace. Naaman didn't have it all figured out when he set out to be healed; he still thought he could buy what he was looking for. When we step out with a longing to follow God faithfully, we won't have all the answers. But once we've experienced the gift of grace, we, like Naaman, can live devoted lives to God, no matter where we go. Just as Naaman carried the soil from Israel home, we carry God's presence with us wherever we go through the gift of the Spirit. We shouldn't overcomplicate what God asks of us and what he offers us. His grace is freely given when we humble ourselves to accept it. Thanks be to God!

Hezekiah

LAYING IT BEFORE GOD

READ 2 KINGS 19

Hezekiah was one of Judah's greatest kings. In fact, 2 Kings 18:5 says, "There was no one like him among all the kings of Judah, either before him or after him." So, what made Hezekiah so special? He had amazing faith and zeal for God.

Hezekiah's father, Ahaz, ranks among Judah's most wicked kings. Ahaz sacrificed his own children in fire (2 Chronicles 28:3). Yet Hezekiah turned away from his father's wicked ways and instead walked according to God's will. His reign began with a grand renewal of proper worship. Hezekiah cleansed the temple, which his father had desecrated. He destroyed the high places and shrines his father had set up for pagan worship. Hezekiah reestablished worship of God in Judah. He invited all of Israel and Judah to celebrate the Passover festival like it had never been celebrated before (2 Chronicles 30).

Hezekiah's greatest test came at the hand of Judah's enemies, the Assyrians. After destroying the Northern Kingdom of Israel, Assyria set its sights on Judah. The Assyrian army began attacking and destroying Judah's towns, eventually laying siege to the capital. From the outside, it appeared Judah was totally outmatched. They couldn't hold a candle to Assyria's military strength.

The Assyrian army commander spat threats and warnings at Hezekiah's men, who relayed the messages to Hezekiah. But rather than panicking or surrendering, Hezekiah went straight to God's temple to pray (2 Kings 19:1). He sent his attendants to talk to the prophet Isaiah. Isaiah sent back a word from the Lord: "Do not be afraid!" (v.6).

Sennacherib, the mighty king of Assyria, then sent Hezekiah a threatening letter, promising to destroy Jerusalem. Still, Hezekiah did not waver. Hezekiah took Sennacherib's letter to God's temple and "spread it out before the LORD" (v. 14). Hezekiah asked God for help, and

God answered in a dramatic way. That night, the angel of God destroyed 185,000 in the Assyrian camp, sending Sennacherib fleeing to Nineveh.

In a fascinating piece of archaeological discovery, scholars have identified and translated Sennacherib's own account of his battles, written in cuneiform on a clay prism.[10] These records agree with the biblical account: The great king of Assyria failed to conquer lowly Jerusalem. Of course, like any politician, Sennacherib tried to spin the story in a favorable way. After listing his victories, he said that, as for Hezekiah, he caged him up in his royal city of Jerusalem like a captive bird. Well, yes, Sennacherib did lay siege to the city—but he didn't win. That's because Hezekiah's strength was in God.

When trials, struggles, or difficult seasons come our way, we can think of that vivid moment where Hezekiah spread Sennacherib's letter before the Lord in the temple. What fear, threat, or uncertainty do you need to lay before God? It might be a big life transition, a difficult medical prognosis, or a tumultuous relationship. As humans, often our first instinct is to panic. Then we either try to solve our problems on our own or we give up and shut down. Neither of these approaches is productive, and they cause an unnecessary world of heartache. Instead, we should follow the model of faithful Hezekiah and lay it before the Lord.

It's important to remember that Hezekiah didn't only turn to God in his most desperate moment, like the proverbial foxhole conversion. Hezekiah had fostered a deep relationship with God throughout his reign, beginning with dismantling the false faith of his father. Hezekiah showed that breaking such sin cycles is indeed possible.

Just as Hezekiah cleansed the temple and rid his kingdom of evil early in his reign, examine your own life and consider where God might be inviting you to experience cleansing through his Word and Spirit.

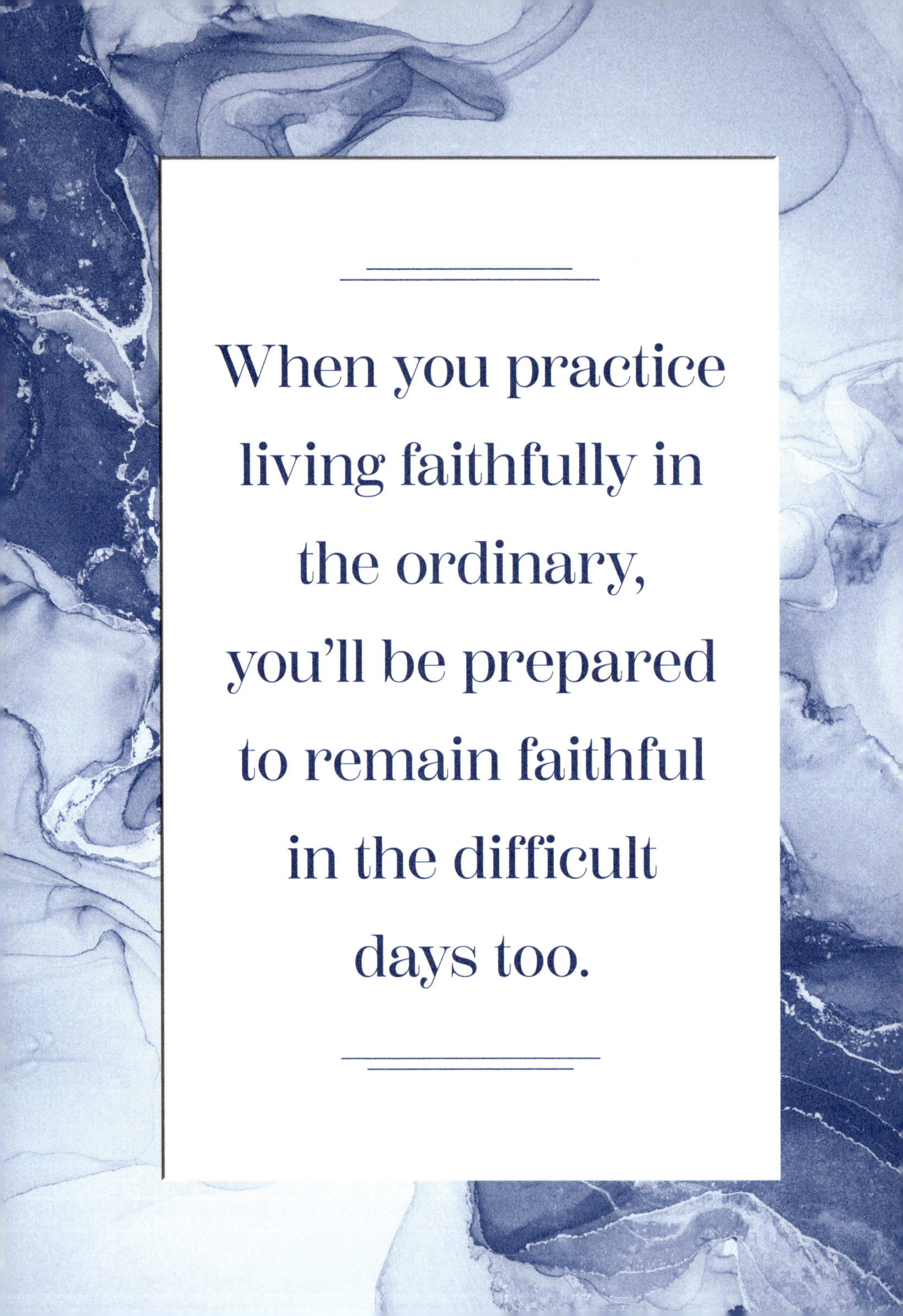
When you practice
living faithfully in
the ordinary,
you'll be prepared
to remain faithful
in the difficult
days too.

Take inventory of your life: What are the God-honoring patterns you want to continue? What are the sins or destructive tendencies you should be careful to avoid?

When you practice living faithfully in the ordinary, you'll be prepared to remain faithful in the difficult days too. As Christ said, "Whoever can be trusted with very little can also be trusted with much" (Luke 16:10). So don't wait till disaster comes. Spread out your life before God and ask for his transforming grace today. Seek God's will even in the ordinary and everyday moments. Then, when troubles come, you won't be shaken.

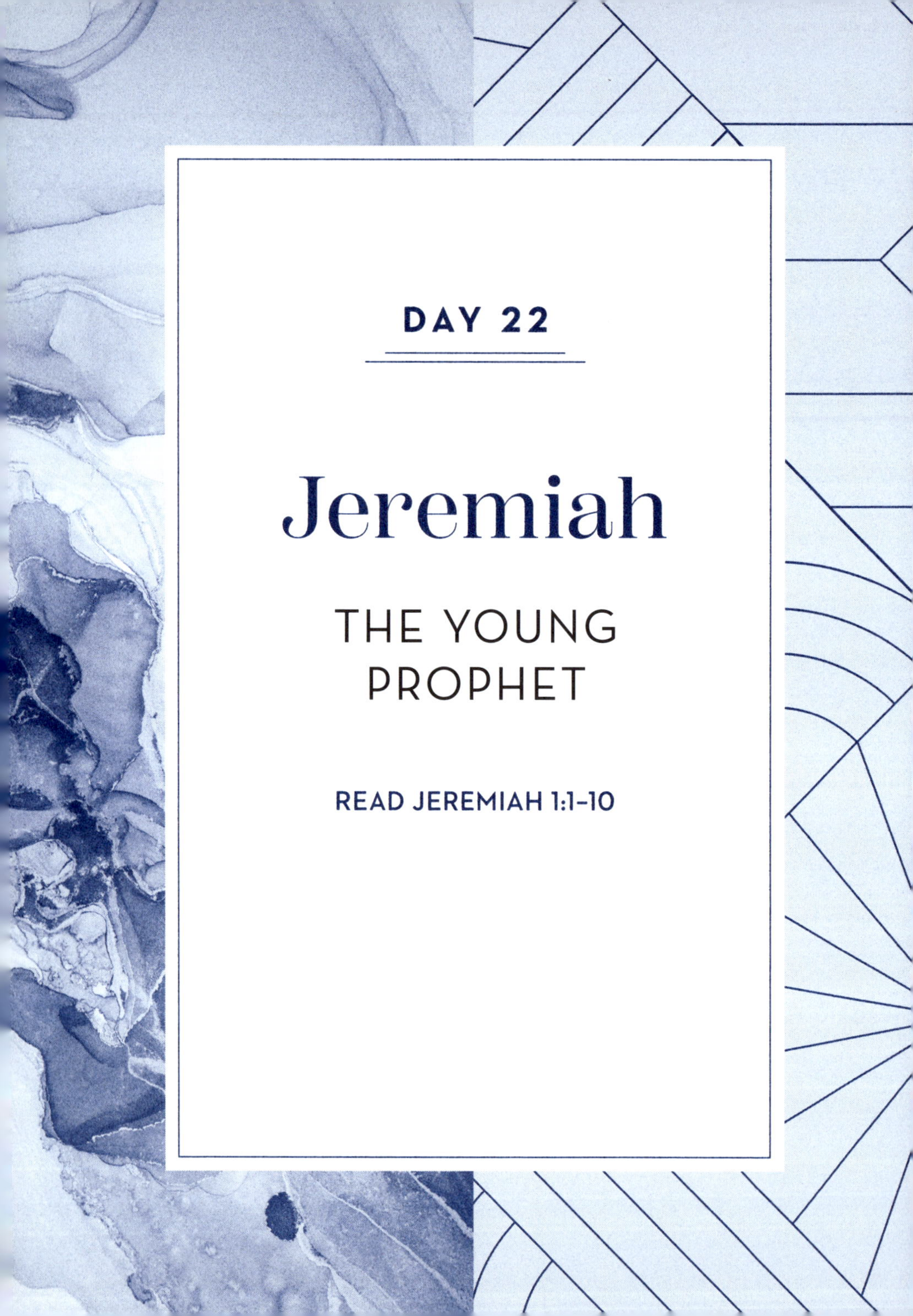

DAY 22

Jeremiah

THE YOUNG PROPHET

READ JEREMIAH 1:1–10

Jeremiah was a prophet during a tumultuous time. His ministry spanned from some of Judah's best days, with the religious reforms of King Josiah, to the ultimate destruction of Jerusalem at the hands of Babylon under King Nebuchadnezzar. Throughout all these years, Jeremiah faithfully obeyed God and delivered his messages to the people of Jerusalem, even when those messages resulted in him being hated and mistreated. Through Jeremiah, we see that speaking God's message of righteousness and justice to those who don't want to hear it will not win us any popularity awards.

The book of Jeremiah (which happens to be the longest book in the Bible by word count) begins with the story of Jeremiah's calling. Jeremiah initially resisted God's call, stating that he did not know how to speak well and was "too young" (1:6). When Jeremiah resisted God's call upon his life, God directed Jeremiah's focus away from his concerns to the truth of God's presence. God assured Jeremiah, "Do not be afraid . . . I am with you and will rescue you" (v. 8). God gave Jeremiah words of comfort and assurance alongside his calling.

There is a story about a pastor who entered the vocation in his mid-twenties, and he felt intimidated at the weight of his calling. One particular visit to a parishioner made him most nervous. It was to an older dutchman, one who made no secret that he thought the "kid preacher" was a little too green.

The young pastor came to visit the elderly member, trusting God to guide the way, and God's Spirit worked throughout the conversation to open the parishioner's eyes to the ministry calling and gifts God had indeed given the young man. When the older man walked the pastor to the door, he shook his hand, looked him in the eye, and said in his Dutch accent, "Thank you for coming, *Dominee*"—a Dutch term for a pastor.

The one who
made us also
equipped us
for serving
his kingdom.

It's a common reflex to excuse and resist God's calling. When we feel God nudging us to a certain task or calling, our first impulse might be to run the other way. This knee-jerk reaction might be because of fear, or it might stem from a sense of our own unworthiness.

The apostle Paul wrote to the young Timothy, "Don't let anyone look down on you because you are young, but set an example for the believers in speech, in conduct, in love, in faith and in purity" (1 Timothy 4:12).

These words aren't only for those of us who are young, but for all of us who feel inadequate. Perhaps we think we lack requisite abilities to be used by God because of our age, status, or experience. Nothing could be further from the truth. The one who made us also equipped us for serving his kingdom.

God's words to Jeremiah should give us tremendous comfort: "Before I formed you in the womb I knew you, before you were born I set you apart" (Jeremiah 1:5). We need to shift our focus from ourselves to the God who made us. He knows better than we do what we are capable of and what he intends for us to do for his kingdom and glory. As Jeremiah himself later reminded God's people, God knows the plans he has for us (29:11).

We don't stand on our own where God calls us to go; God is with us. Like Jeremiah, we can strive to be faithful to our callings in good times and bad. What has God called you to do? Who has God made you to be? He will certainly equip you. Turn from what you don't think you can do to the one who makes all things possible, who has called you according to his good purposes. The God who made us has certainly equipped us to walk in those plans. We have all we need.

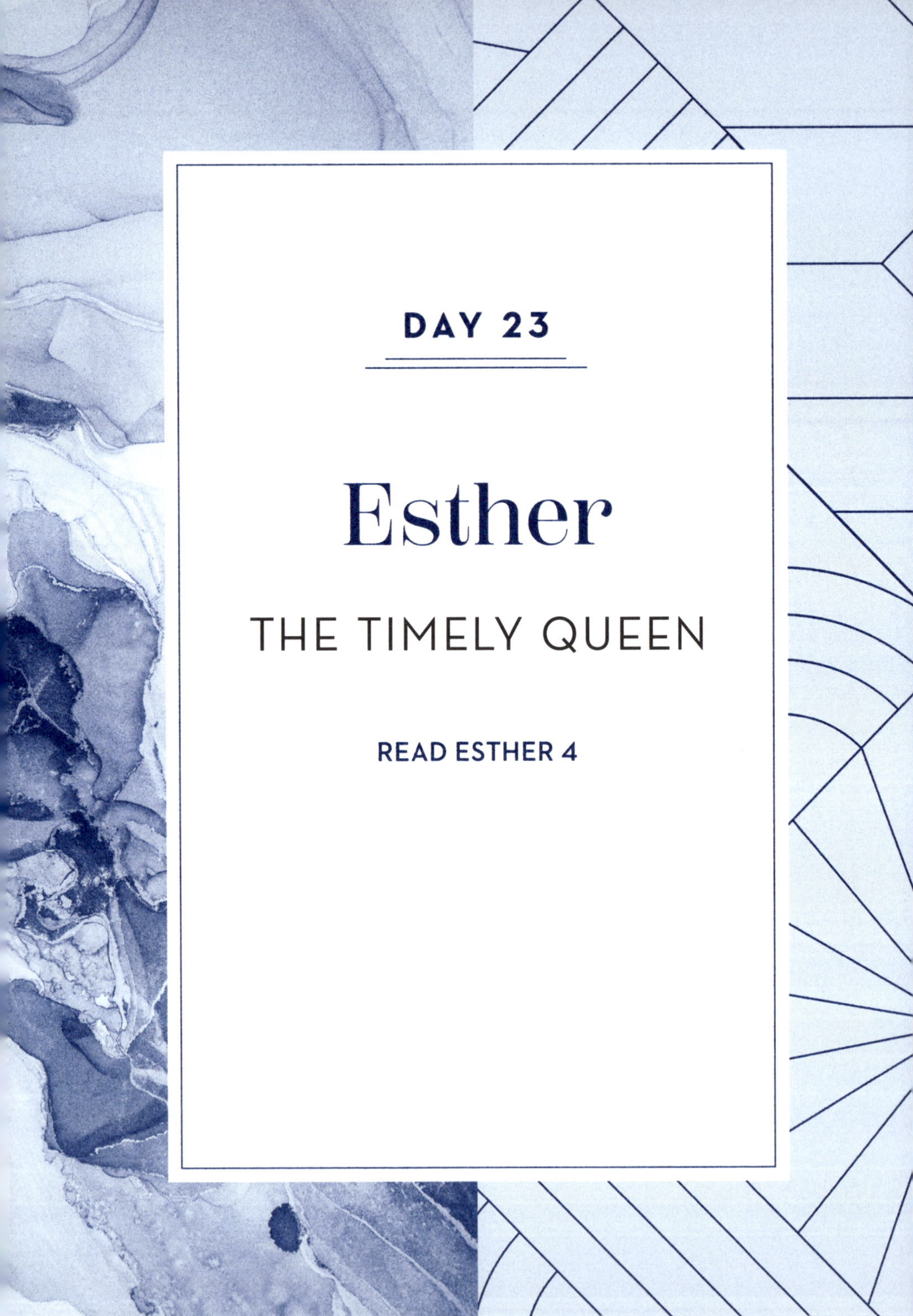

DAY 23

Esther

THE TIMELY QUEEN

READ ESTHER 4

Olga Crommelin was just a teenager when she risked her life to save a young Jewish boy from being taken by Nazi soldiers. The boy, Arnold Van Den Berg, was only two years old. His parents lived in hiding in the home of a Dutch family, but little Arnold was too much of a liability. Any noise he made when Nazi soldiers checked the home would give the family's hiding place away, resulting in their removal to a concentration camp. To keep both family and child safe, Olga took young Arnold to a village where she placed him in an orphanage with a few other Jewish children. On the way, she had to walk with this Jewish toddler right past a group of Nazis.

Arnold and his parents survived the war, were reunited, and eventually emigrated to California. Years later, Arnold still grappled with understanding why teenage Olga would risk her life to save him, a baby she didn't even know. As he processed this question in therapy, Arnold's psychologist pointed out that when a person's principles are more important than their life, that person will risk their life for the sake of what they believe is right.[11] There are times when standing up for justice is so important that you will risk your own life to do it. Esther's story illustrates the same truth.

The crisis in the book of Esther began when Haman, the Persian king Xerxes' right-hand man, convinced the king to issue an edict demanding the genocide of all the Jews. Xerxes was unaware that his own queen, Esther, was herself Jewish. Upon hearing that her cousin Mordecai, who had raised her, was in mourning, Esther sent a messenger to find out what was wrong, and Mordecai, explaining the threat, urged her to intercede for her people. Esther resisted, noting that anyone who approached the king unsummoned—even the queen herself—could be put to death. Yet Mordecai was adamant, saying,

"Who knows but that you have come to your royal position for such a time as this?" (4:14).

Esther responded to Mordecai's words with bold courage. Though she knew it could mean her own death, she resolved to go before the king on behalf of her people: "If I perish, I perish" (v. 16). Like Olga Crommelin, Esther understood that there are times when standing up for justice, even if it means risking your own life, is the right thing to do. Like other faithful people we have read about thus far, Esther was prepared to lay down her life for the sake of others. In this way, her story points toward the self-giving sacrifice of Christ on the cross.

Perhaps you have noticed that the book of Esther never mentions God. This makes it a fascinating study in finding God at work even when the Bible writer does not tell us exactly what God is doing, or why. This is a skill we must exercise in our own lives. God doesn't usually tell us clearly what he's doing in our life circumstances and challenges. Instead, we must calibrate our vision to see God at work in the everyday.

Mordecai's powerful words offer us a standard for this calibration. Why has God put you where you are? Is there a neighbor or a coworker—perhaps someone who has no one else who knows their situation quite like you do—whom God might be calling you to bless or care for? What resources or talents has God given you that you can use to enhance the ministry of God's kingdom in your community? God is a master arranger of people, circumstances, and timing. Let Mordecai's words challenge you. God has put you where you are "for such a time as this." The way we live our lives impacts the lives of others. Keep your mind and heart open to why God has placed you where you are in this moment.

Our everyday choices and actions have real justice implications. Esther's story should lead us to take these implications seriously. Who

There are times when standing up for justice, even if it means risking your own life, is the right thing to do.

are the people around us who need our prayers and our acts of selfless love? Who are the people far away whose lives we might be able to impact through support of worthy organizations or wiser consumer habits? Christ said those who hunger and thirst for righteousness and justice (Greek, *dikaiosune*) are blessed (Matthew 5:6). Our hearts and lives should be attentive to the hunger and thirst of such people, who are honored in God's eyes. Like Esther, we must faithfully stand up for justice, looking with God's perspective to find why we have been placed where we are. Pray for God to help you with this worthy task today.

DAY 24

Daniel

A FAITHFUL EXILE

READ DANIEL 6

You may have had the pleasure of attending a performance of Handel's *Messiah* or hearing it on the radio at Christmastime. It is a beautiful and intricate piece. One of the movements declares this about Christ, "He trusted in God that He would deliver Him; let Him deliver Him, if He delight in Him."[12] These words come from Psalm 22:8, but they could just as well be the words of King Darius to Daniel: "May your God, whom you serve continually, rescue you!" (Daniel 6:16). As we find in Daniel's story, that's exactly what God did.

Daniel had been taken captive from Jerusalem when Babylon conquered the city under King Nebuchadnezzar. The Babylonians dragged all the middle- and upper-class people hundreds of miles east, to Babylon. Daniel and other young men like him were conscripted into the king's service. They were taught the language and culture of Babylon, given new names, and stripped of their old identities. At least that was the idea.

Daniel showed that while the Babylonians could take him out of Jerusalem, they could not take the faith he learned in Jerusalem out of him. Daniel was committed to God. He prayed three times a day, always facing the direction of Jerusalem, though it was destroyed and far beyond the western horizon. We can perhaps imagine Daniel singing the mournful song preserved for us as Psalm 137: "May my tongue cling to the roof of my mouth if I do not remember you, if I do not consider Jerusalem my highest joy" (v. 6). A foreign land, a new name, and a new vocation as an officer to the king could not take away Daniel's faith. Whatever was taken away from Daniel, Daniel never let go of his trust in God.

Daniel's special giftedness for royal service led the king to favor him above his other officials, which caused those officials to burn with envy against Daniel. Knowing King Darius intended to make Daniel

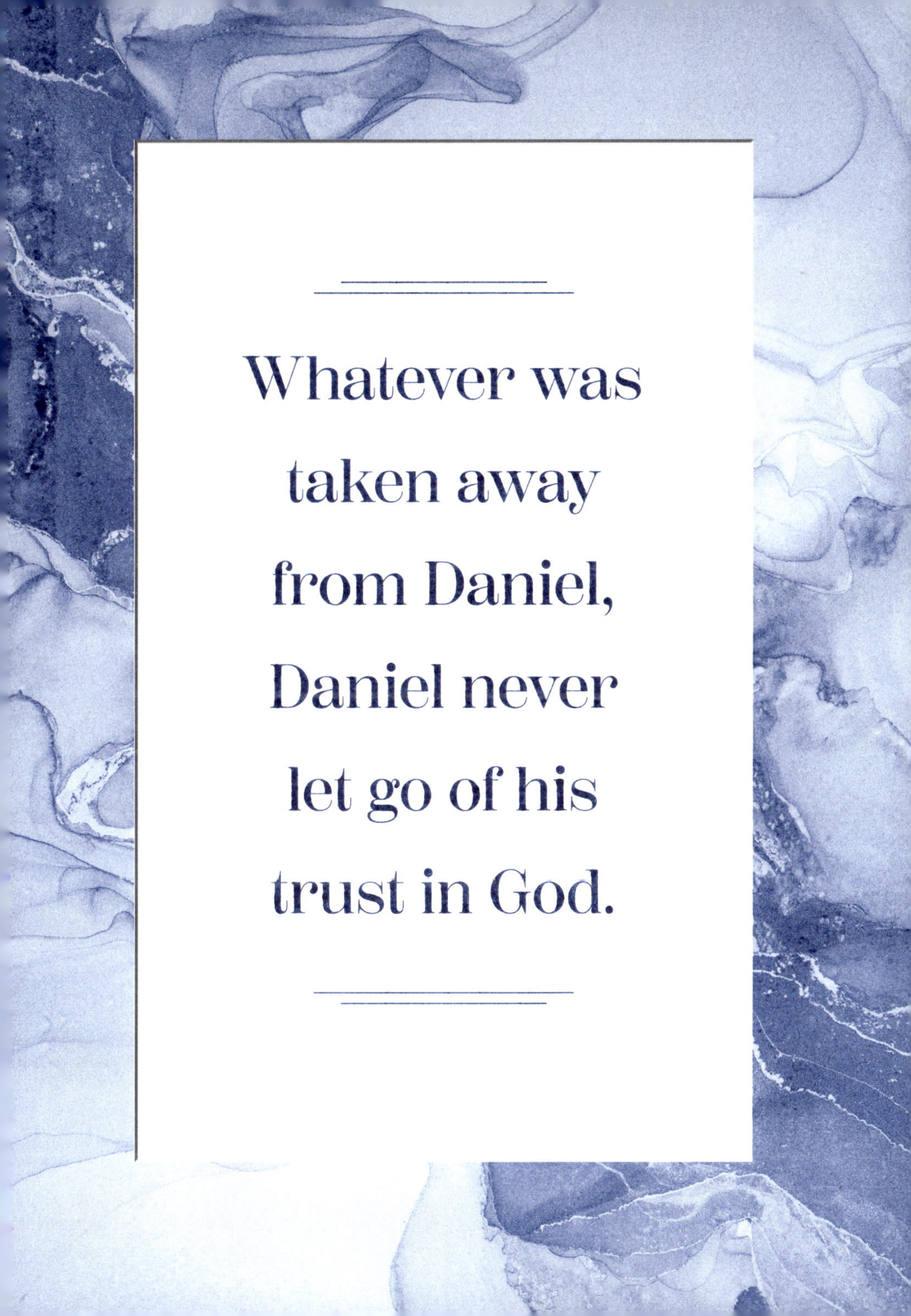
Whatever was
taken away
from Daniel,
Daniel never
let go of his
trust in God.

his highest official, the others sought some grounds to accuse Daniel of wrongdoing. The problem was, Daniel was above reproach. He had no skeletons in his closet, no corruption or negligence of duty with which the other officials could make a case against him. Can you imagine a politician with such a spotless record? Daniel embodied the words of 1 Peter 2:12: "Live such good lives among the pagans that, though they accuse you of doing wrong, they may see your good deeds and glorify God on the day he visits us."

Far from glorifying Daniel's God, however, his adversaries took a different approach. They convinced Darius to make a law prohibiting worship of anyone or anything other than Darius for thirty days. When Daniel learned about the law, he didn't despair, and he certainly didn't bend to the king's demands. He simply walked straight to his room and prayed.

King Darius's officials had him in a bind, and he was forced to send Daniel to the lions' den for his disregard of the law. That's when Darius told Daniel, "May your God, whom you serve continually, rescue you!" (Daniel 6:16). And, of course, that's exactly what God did: "No wound was found on him, because he had trusted in his God" (v. 23). As a result, King Darius himself was moved to profess faith in Daniel's God: "He is the living God and he endures forever. . . . He rescues and he saves" (vv. 26–27). Daniel's faithfulness to God led the king of Babylon to praise God's name.

Daniel's story reminds us that we should always seek to live lives that are beyond reproach. Our Monday through Saturday conduct must not be out of sync with our Sunday worship. We should seek to live, by God's grace and the sanctifying presence of God's Spirit, blameless lives in this world, remembering Christ's words: "Let your light shine before others, that they may see your good deeds and glorify your Father in heaven" (Matthew 5:16). Daniel modeled this: His faithfulness to God led Darius to glorify God.

Examine your heart and life. Have you grown lukewarm in your love for God and in your desire to follow Christ? What circumstances may have led to this? Take inspiration from Daniel's faithfulness. Removed from everything he knew, and also given the luxury of a royal position, he nonetheless remained anchored to God. Losing much must not lead us away from God, and neither should gaining much. As Job declared, the Lord gives and the Lord takes away (Job 1:21). Our task is to remain faithful in hope and in prayer in every circumstance, putting our ultimate trust in God. When we trust in God, we'll find again and again that he will indeed deliver us.

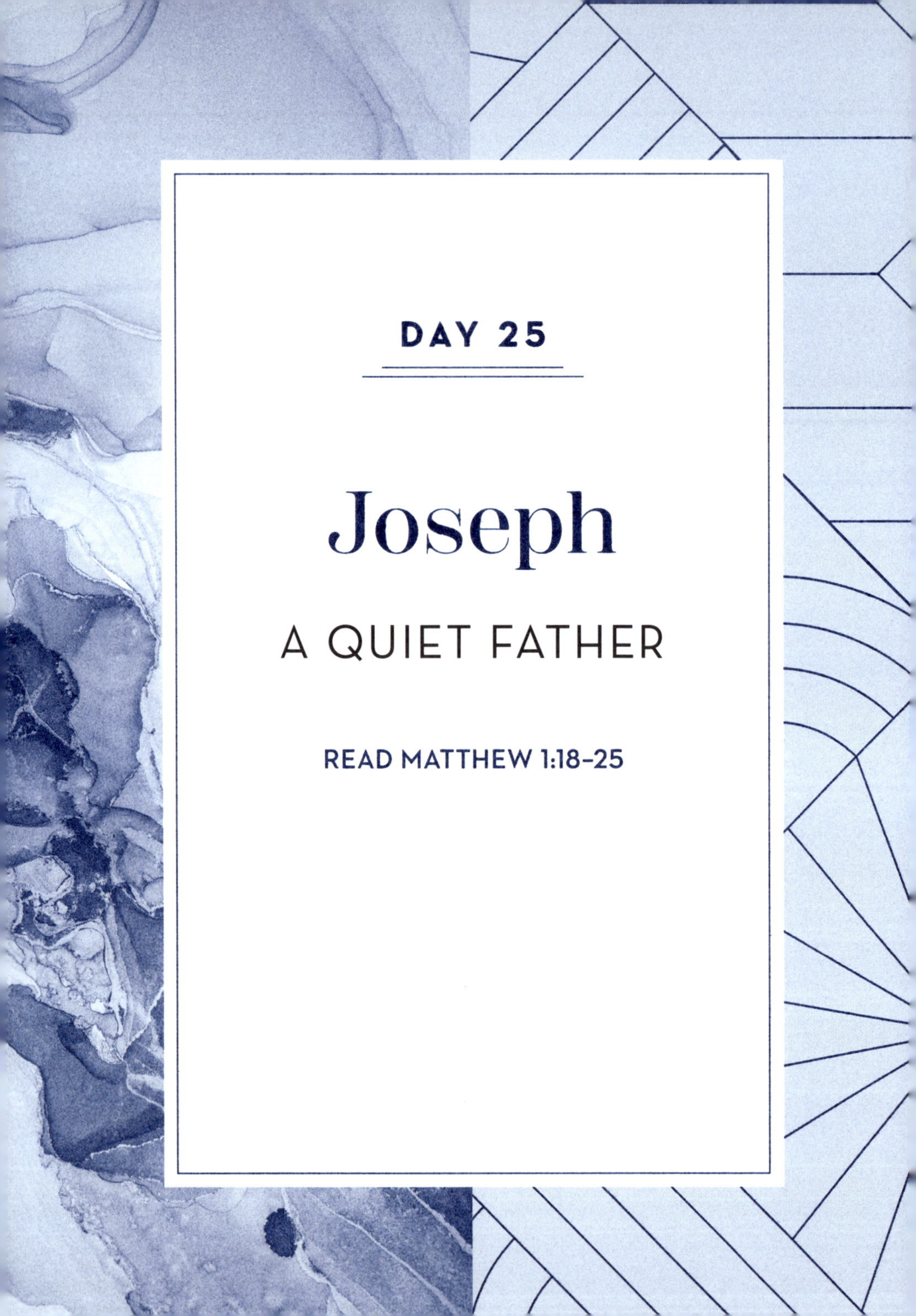

DAY 25

Joseph

A QUIET FATHER

READ MATTHEW 1:18–25

In many organizations, there are quiet people working behind the scenes who don't get much credit or attention but who are integral for everything to work smoothly. I have found, working in churches, that often the office administrator has a better finger on the pulse of the pastoral needs in the congregation than anyone else. Yet people rarely view this person as a primary resource for the church's spiritual needs. Sometimes it is the quiet and unassuming people who have the most important roles. Joseph, the husband of Mary, was a person like this.

Joseph probably had a fairly humble vision for his future. He would marry a young woman named Mary, the two would settle down, he would work his trade, and they would raise a family in the region of Galilee. Things were moving smoothly in this quaint direction until the unthinkable happened. While Mary and Joseph were still engaged, he found out Mary was pregnant.

Breaking off an engagement wasn't as simple then as it is today. Joseph couldn't just ask for the engagement ring back so the two could move on in separate directions. No, breaking out of their engagement would require a formal divorce. And this caused Joseph some anguish. He had valid grounds for this divorce: Mary was pregnant, after all, and he knew he had nothing to do with it. But divorcing Mary on the grounds of committing adultery would mean Mary could be put to death—at the very least, it would subject her to a lifetime of shame and disgrace.

The Bible says Joseph was faithful to the law, yet he did not want to expose Mary to public disgrace. He sought to uphold the standards of God's law, but also wanted to obey God by showing mercy. He wanted to live the truth while being full of grace. Because of this, he decided to divorce Mary quietly, rather than making the issue a public spectacle. Joseph seems to have embodied Paul's exhortation in Ephesians 4:2:

"Be completely humble and gentle; be patient, bearing with one another in love."

Seeking to deal with the situation quietly suited Joseph's character, at least as far as we know. The fact is, the Bible never records a single word from Joseph. In the narrative, he's a quiet servant of God.

Not all of God's servants are gifted to be preachers, teachers, or evangelists. Not all of God's people will lead Bible studies or use many words at all. For many, gifting comes in quieter forms—but this does not make their service any less noble or God-glorifying. God delights in humble servants.

Before Joseph could act on his divorce plans, God sent an angel to him in a dream. The angel told him not to be afraid to take Mary as his wife. The child she was bearing was conceived not by another man but by the Holy Spirit. Her child would be a son, the angel told Joseph, and that son would be named Jesus, "because he will save his people from their sins" (Matthew 1:21).

Now, put yourself in Joseph's shoes for a moment. You have this dramatic dream in which an angel speaks to you. On the one hand, you know from the stories of your faith that dreams ought to be taken seriously. On the other hand, you might think it was only a dream. It did sound, after all, quite unbelievable. So what would you do?

The Bible says Joseph simply obeyed. He did not ask questions. He did not resist God's calling, as many other people in the Bible often did. Joseph's response was completely matter-of-fact: "When Joseph woke up, he did what the angel of the Lord had commanded him and took Mary home as his wife" (v. 24).

Joseph's witness to us is in his faithful and quiet obedience. This dream and this child guaranteed that Joseph's life would not be what

God delights
in humble
servants.

he envisioned, and yet he yielded his life and his future to God. What a difficult lesson this can be for us to learn! So often, we make plans that we grow too attached to. We use pros and cons lists and factor in any number of considerations, and then we set out resolutely toward our imagined future. Our hope isn't for God to show us his plans, but rather for God to bless *our* plans. This is the wrong approach. Our hearts must stay open to God's guidance.

When you think of people whose faith you look up to and have been inspired by, what are the qualities they possess that attract you and earn your respect? Is it sure knowledge and gifts for speaking? While we may be inspired by certain preachers who possess wonderful gifts of using words to make God's love seem so present and alive, often it is the faith of people like Joseph we should look to as an example. Pay attention to the people in your life with a quiet faith, a humble faith, who obey with a simple trust, even in moments of uncertainty. A quiet faithfulness, like Joseph's, speaks volumes about God.

Mary

A MIGHTY MOTHER

READ LUKE 1:39–56

We have already looked at a number of people in the Bible whose lives God abruptly interrupted and set on a new course. Yet, perhaps no interruption was as dramatic and life-altering as the one Mary experienced. The angel Gabriel appeared to Mary while she was engaged to Joseph and told her she would give birth to a son who would be called Son of the Most High and who would rule on David's throne (Luke 1:32).

Mary was a young woman from the region of Galilee, quite likely a teenager. The Bible doesn't give the impression that she came from a remarkable family, and the fact that she and Joseph offered two birds as a sacrifice when Jesus was presented at the temple indicates that Mary and Joseph were poor (Luke 2:24; Leviticus 12:8). God didn't choose Mary because of high status. Mary did, however, demonstrate immense faith. She did not resist God's calling, just like many other people in the Bible (Moses, Gideon, Jeremiah, and more). Instead, she asked just one practical question: "How will this be . . . since I am a virgin?" (Luke 1:34).

Gabriel explained that God's Holy Spirit would conceive the child in Mary's womb. As a testimony of the miraculous power of God, Gabriel told Mary that her own cousin Elizabeth, who was elderly and who had been unable to conceive, was herself in her sixth month of pregnancy. Remarkable as this was, I imagine that you or I would still have had some questions or concerns for Gabriel. Mary, however, received God's word with complete acceptance and faith: "I am the Lord's servant. . . . May your word to me be fulfilled" (v. 38).

Like Joseph, Mary responded to God's unbelievable message with humble trust. Those of us who are planners or worriers should be encouraged by Mary's story to trust in God's plans rather than our own. And when God reveals that he has something very different in store

Those of us who are planners or worriers should be encouraged by Mary's story to trust in God's plans rather than our own.

from what we expected, we should step forward with faithful acceptance, like Mary.

While Joseph is not mentioned during Jesus' adult ministry, Mary remained with Jesus even until his death. At the wedding feast in Cana, she already showed an awareness of his power (John 2:3–5). Mary was even present on the day of Pentecost when God's Spirit was unleashed upon the church (Acts 1:14). She was able to see Jesus not only as her son, but also as the Son of God and the Savior of the world.

Mary's story is exceptional, but in another sense, it is not unique among God's children. Mary was called to carry Jesus in her womb, to give birth to the Word-made-flesh. We are to spiritually carry out this same calling, bearing the Word in our lives by faith and by God's Spirit. God's children today, who carry the life of Christ within us, should declare what we know to be true of God. Like Mary, our hearts should overflow with gratitude and praise. Our lives should become a hymn proclaiming God's grace and power.

How have you experienced God's mercy upon you? Where has God opened up new paths or plans for you, things you didn't expect or anticipate? Thank God in prayer and proclaim his goodness to others as a witness to his grace in your life.

DAY 27

Peter

THE ROCK OF FAITH

READ MATTHEW 16:13–20

There are quite literally thousands of Christian denominations in the world, and we are well aware that they don't all get along or even respect one another. You have likely heard a member of one Christian church disparage the faith or practice of believers in another Christian church. Perhaps they accused the other of being too liberal or too traditional, of focusing on social justice at the expense of doctrine, or of being more focused on dogma than on living out the love of Christ. Maybe they just didn't like the music style in the other church, or they accused the church of being inhospitable. Christians have found seemingly countless reasons to separate from one another over the centuries. It begs the question: What is it that holds Christians together, if anything at all? What is the rock the Christian faith is built upon, across all its diverse communities?

The earliest creed in the Christian church was the simple declaration that "Jesus is Lord." In a Roman world that declared Caesar to be lord, this Christian creed had political implications. Christians were not people of the empire; they were people of God. They didn't place their hope in political or elected officials; they put their hope in Christ. The apostle Peter was the first of Christ's followers to make that declaration of faith: "You are the Messiah, the Son of the living God" (Matthew 16:16). Consider for a moment what an astounding claim this was for Peter to make. Peter had been called to follow a rabbi, a Jewish teacher. Rabbis frequently called disciples to follow them; this was not original to Jesus. Yet Peter understood something deeper: Jesus was no ordinary rabbi; he was the very Son of God.

Peter made this powerful profession when Jesus asked his disciples, "Who do people say the Son of Man is?" (v. 13). The disciples offered some answers they must have overheard from the crowds that so often followed Jesus. Some, they told him, claimed Jesus was John the Baptist returned from the dead. Others thought he was one of the great prophets of old, maybe even Jeremiah or Elijah. Clearly, the people marveled at Jesus, thinking he might be a prophet returned from the dead.

But then Jesus asked the more important question: "But what about you? . . . Who do you say I am?" (v. 15). This is the question we all need to answer. Who do you say Jesus is?

C. S. Lewis famously suggested that people offer three kinds of answers to this question. Some say that Jesus was a liar. He led the people along, allowing them to think he was something greater than he really was, even encouraging them in a delusion. Lewis said others might say Jesus was a lunatic. He believed what he said, but he was crazy. But neither accounts for Jesus' miracles, witnessed and proclaimed by so many who died professing their belief that he was Lord.

In the end, Lewis wrote that if we reject Jesus as a liar and a lunatic, we must confess Jesus was and is Lord.[13] Now, this provides a nice apologetic framework for Christians discussing Jesus. But each one of us needs to answer Jesus' question in our own personal way. Jesus' question to his disciples speaks from the pages of Scripture to us today: Who do *you* say Jesus is?

Peter's answer—that Jesus is the Messiah and the Son of God—caused Jesus to say to him, "This was not revealed to you by flesh and blood, but by my Father in heaven" (v. 17). Jesus went on to tell Peter, "You are Peter, and on this rock I will build my church, and the gates of Hades will not overcome it" (v. 18). Christians have debated how to understand the "rock" upon which Jesus said he would build his church. Is the rock Peter himself? Certainly Peter was a monumental figure in the early church, the disciple who delivered the powerful Pentecost

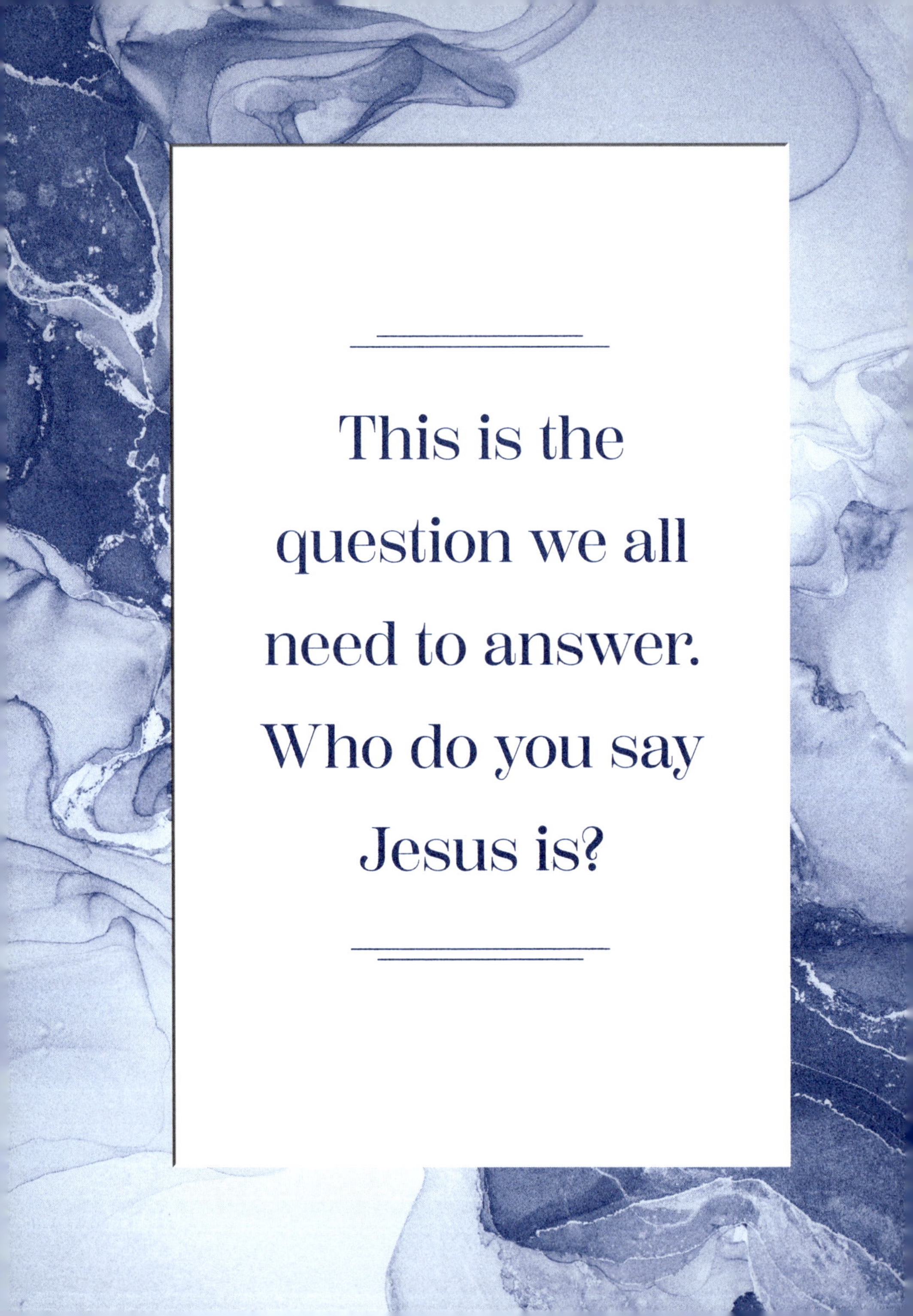
This is the question we all need to answer. Who do you say Jesus is?

sermon that God used to supercharge the community of Christ followers (Acts 2:14–41).

At the same time, the rock upon which Christ said he would build his church was more likely Peter's confession itself: that Jesus is the Messiah, the Son of God. This is the belief that became the earliest creed of the church: Jesus is Lord. And in all the diverse communities of the church today, this remains the central creed. It's the confession that each believer, following after Peter, must make—that Jesus is Lord. When this is our creed, Christ promises that even the gates of hell itself cannot overcome his church.

DAY 28

Mary Magdalene

A WITNESS TO THE RESURRECTION

READ JOHN 20:1–18

Mary Magdalene was one of several women who devotedly followed Jesus not only during his ministry in the northern region of Galilee but also to the point of his death and resurrection. In fact, John's gospel tells the story of the resurrected Jesus appearing to Mary Magdalene before he appeared to any of the other disciples.

Mary's background must have been painful and difficult. Luke 8:2 tells us that Jesus had cast seven demons out of Mary. She is listed among the women who helped support Jesus and his disciples "out of their own means" (v. 3).

While Mary's demons certainly suggest a troubled past before coming to Christ, it is also true that church history and tradition have not been fair to Mary. For many centuries, Mary has been confused and identified with the "sinful woman" (probably a prostitute) in Luke 7:36–50. The Bible does not say, however, that Mary was this woman. Though Jesus showed grace and mercy to that sinful woman—and so we must not disparage her either but rather see her in light of God's grace—we should avoid perpetuating the unfounded belief that Mary was a prostitute.

Several of the women who followed Jesus remained with him to the point of his death on the cross, even while many of his male disciples scattered. Mary Magdalene is listed along with Mary the mother of Jesus and Mary the wife of Clopas as being present at Jesus' final moments, along with the disciple John (John 19:25–26).

Scripture tells us Mary went to anoint Jesus' body first thing Sunday morning but found the stone of the tomb rolled away and the tomb itself empty. She hurried to tell Simon Peter and John, who went to see for themselves before going back to where they were staying. Mary, however, remained at Christ's tomb, weeping. When the risen Christ appeared to her, Mary first thought he was the gardener and asked if he had placed Jesus' body somewhere. It was not until Jesus spoke her name that her eyes were opened to the presence of her risen Lord before her.

Jesus gave Mary a mission to go tell the other disciples about him. What a gift! Mary was the first person entrusted with the life-saving message of Christ's resurrection. She was the first person to announce to the world that Jesus had risen from the dead. She ran again to the disciples, this time with joy rather than despair, and told them, "I have seen the Lord!" (John 20:18).

We can only imagine what the seven demons in Mary's life had done to her before they were cast out, but it was certainly a dark reality. Perhaps, like with Saul in the Old Testament, these bad spirits caused her depression and mental anguish. When Christ came into her life, she was set free. She devoted herself fully to following him.

The same story should be true for us. Some believers today have conversions just as dramatic as Mary's, where God frees them from the demonic grip of darkness. For others, their story of coming to new life in Christ might not seem so dramatic. But really, there is no difference. The only thing that matters—the reality that shines through every story of salvation—is that God's grace brings a person out of darkness and into the light of Christ (1 Peter 2:9). God does this so that we might proclaim his praise and tell the world what he has done for us in Christ.

A beautiful moment in Mary's encounter with Jesus is when he calls her by her name. This is the moment she sees that it is truly Christ before her. God knows his people by name, and he calls them by name throughout the Bible (Abraham, Moses, Samuel, Paul, and more). Christ

Our faith is not based on abstract statements about God; it's anchored in our own experience of God coming to us and calling us.

is like the shepherding gatekeeper who "calls his own sheep by name" (John 10:3). Our faith is not based on abstract statements about God; it's anchored in our own experience of God coming to us and calling us. His voice and grace are unmistakable. When we hear him, we follow, and we proclaim his saving love to the world.

Mary's mission from Christ to tell others about the risen Lord is the mission of the entire church. Before he ascended, Jesus told his disciples, "You will be my witnesses" (Acts 1:8). Living faithfully to Christ means bearing witness in our actions and in our speech to the resurrection of Jesus Christ. Once we come to know Jesus, we, like Mary, should follow him relentlessly, wherever he leads, always telling the world the good news of his resurrection and salvation.

DAY 29

Matthew

PARTY HOST FOR SINNERS

READ LUKE 5:27–32

Many Christians live with a nagging sense of guilt or apprehension about the New Testament's call to tell the world about Jesus. Yes, we know we should be spreading the gospel—but how? It's daunting to invite people to church, and perhaps we suspect that our coworkers and neighbors wouldn't feel like they fit in well at our churches. Not sure what to do, we might be tempted to give up and leave the evangelism to people who have that "gift." While evangelism is certainly a gift (Ephesians 4:11), spreading the good news about Jesus is the task of every believer. So, how do we do it? The disciple Matthew offered us a helpful method.

Matthew, also called Levi, was a tax collector. The Jewish people in Jesus' day hated tax collectors for taking their money and giving it to the Roman government. Tax collectors were regarded as traitors to their own people. They also had a reputation for gouging people with higher tax bills than necessary to skim off a bit for themselves. Suffice it to say, no one would have considered a tax collector to be worthy disciple material for a Jewish rabbi. No one, that is, except Jesus.

Seeing Matthew in his tax booth one day, Jesus issued the same invitation he had given to the fishermen who became his disciples: "Follow me" (Luke 5:27). Though others looked at Matthew as an outcast, Jesus saw in him someone who could become a faithful follower. Matthew left everything and followed.

Then Matthew did a wonderful thing. He threw a banquet, inviting all his old acquaintances and accomplices, people considered "sinners." This was a big party for Jesus. The Bible says there was a "large crowd" of these tax collectors and sinners; it was not a small gathering (v. 29). The religious leaders complained to Jesus' disciples about his participation at this gathering. They would never deign to eat with such despicable types! They asked, "Why do you eat and drink with tax collectors and sinners?" (v. 30). Jesus told them it was not the healthy who needed a doctor but the sick. He had come to call sinners to repentance, and that meant spending time with them.

Bringing your nonbelieving neighbor to a church service might be a lot to start with (though we should never underestimate how God's Spirit can move!). Maybe God is calling you to offer an easier on-ramp for the people in your life who don't yet know the Lord. Why not host a "Matthew party"? Just as Matthew invited all his friends to a party with Jesus, we can invite people we know to spend time with us and others who already know Christ. Who knows what seeds might be planted in such gatherings?

Some of us were blessed to grow up in homes where our Christian faith was nourished. Perhaps you professed your faith in church early in your life by walking up front and giving your life to Jesus. Others of us came to faith as adults through friends who cared for us, supported us, and who were also unapologetic about their love for Jesus. Like Jesus with tax collectors and sinners, those friends became part of our journey, investing time and energy into building meaningful relationships with us.

We are called to follow in the ministry of Jesus. If we are going to look and live like Jesus, this means we also need to be intentional about reaching beyond the walls of our churches. We need to go out and meet people, building relationships with them, and gathering with them as Jesus did.

Of course, we must always conduct ourselves in a way that reflects positively on Christ, whom we represent. But we cannot simply build churches and hope people will show up. God's people need to go out

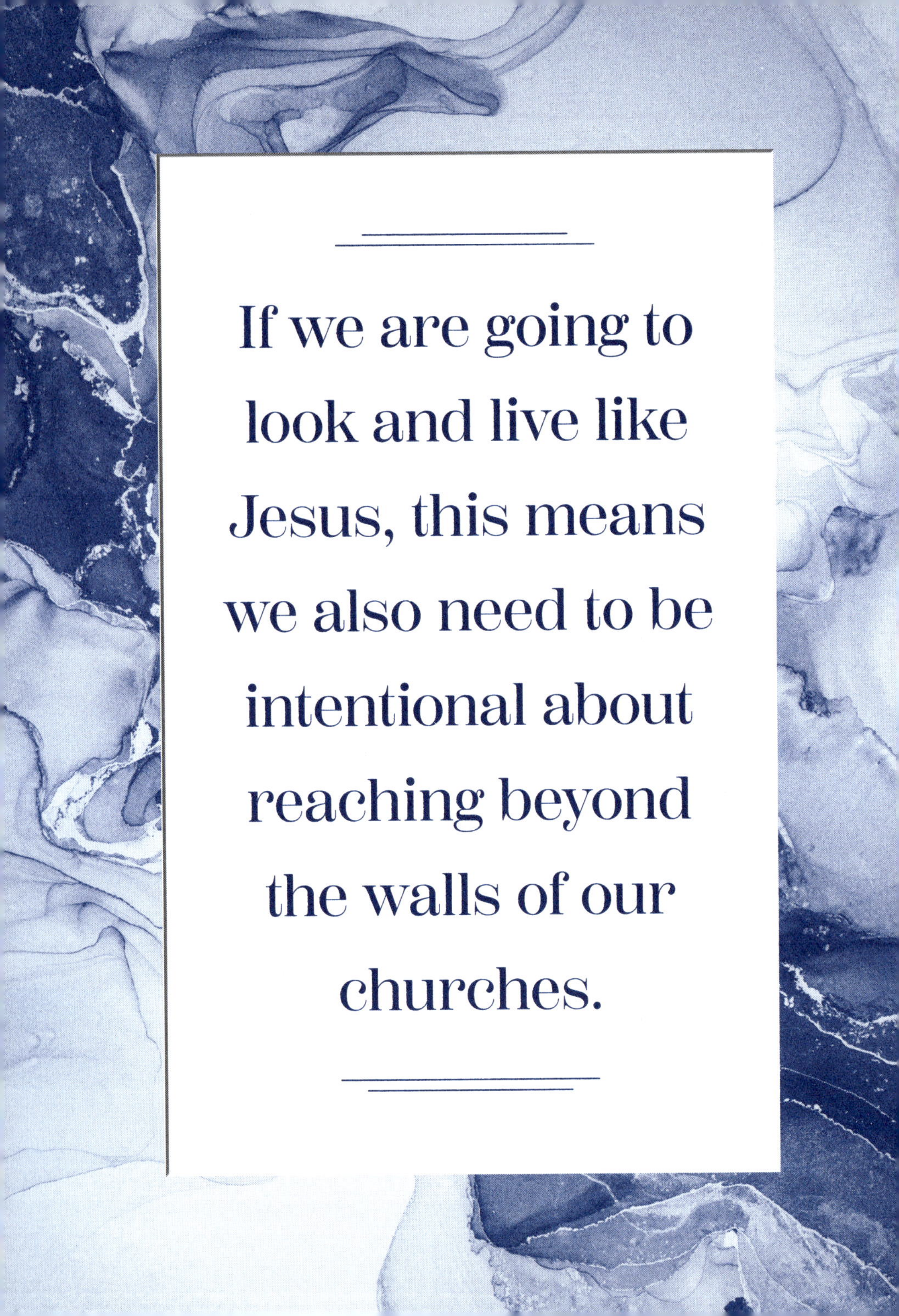
If we are going to look and live like Jesus, this means we also need to be intentional about reaching beyond the walls of our churches.

and practice following Jesus with real people who don't know him yet. Though it is Christ who does the saving, by his grace and Spirit he uses his people to reach out and spread the gospel. Isaiah 40:4 proclaims a time when "the rough ground shall become level, the rugged places a plain." God's followers can make the rough journey from unbelief to faith a little smoother for those around us by showing our Christian faith through our love (John 13:35).

DAY 30

The Samaritan Woman

FROM SHAME TO EVANGELIST

READ JOHN 4:1–42

Christ's encounter with the Samaritan woman has long been one of my favorite conversations recorded in the Bible. The scene is set as Jesus traveled north with his disciples from Judea back to his home territory of Galilee. Between these two Jewish regions was territory inhabited by the Samaritans, a group of people the Jews did not care for (John 4:9). Samaritans were considered heretics, descendants of the northern tribes of Israel who had married Gentile neighbors. The Jews, on the other hand, were descendants of the Southern Kingdom of Judah and prided themselves on not having intermarried with their neighbors. When Jews journeyed between the regions of Galilee and Judea, they often crossed over the Jordan River rather than going straight through the Samaritan territory, preferring a longer trip over encountering Samaritans.

Yet Jesus took the direct route. He led the disciples to the Samaritan town of Sychar, where they left him to go find food. Jesus waited at Jacob's well, and around noon, a woman came to draw water. The time is significant. Women drawing water would usually come early in the morning. The fact that this woman was drawing water in the heat of the day indicates that she didn't want to encounter the other women in town.

Jesus began the conversation innocently enough, asking for some water—though the fact that a Jewish rabbi would talk to a Samaritan woman at all was quite a surprise to her. Jesus went on to tell her that he could offer her living water, "a spring of water welling up to eternal life" (v. 14). The woman was intrigued. But then Jesus abruptly changed the subject: "Go, call your husband and come back" (v. 16).

Immediately her shame set in. Jesus knew what he was doing and revealed that he knew everything about her. She'd had five husbands

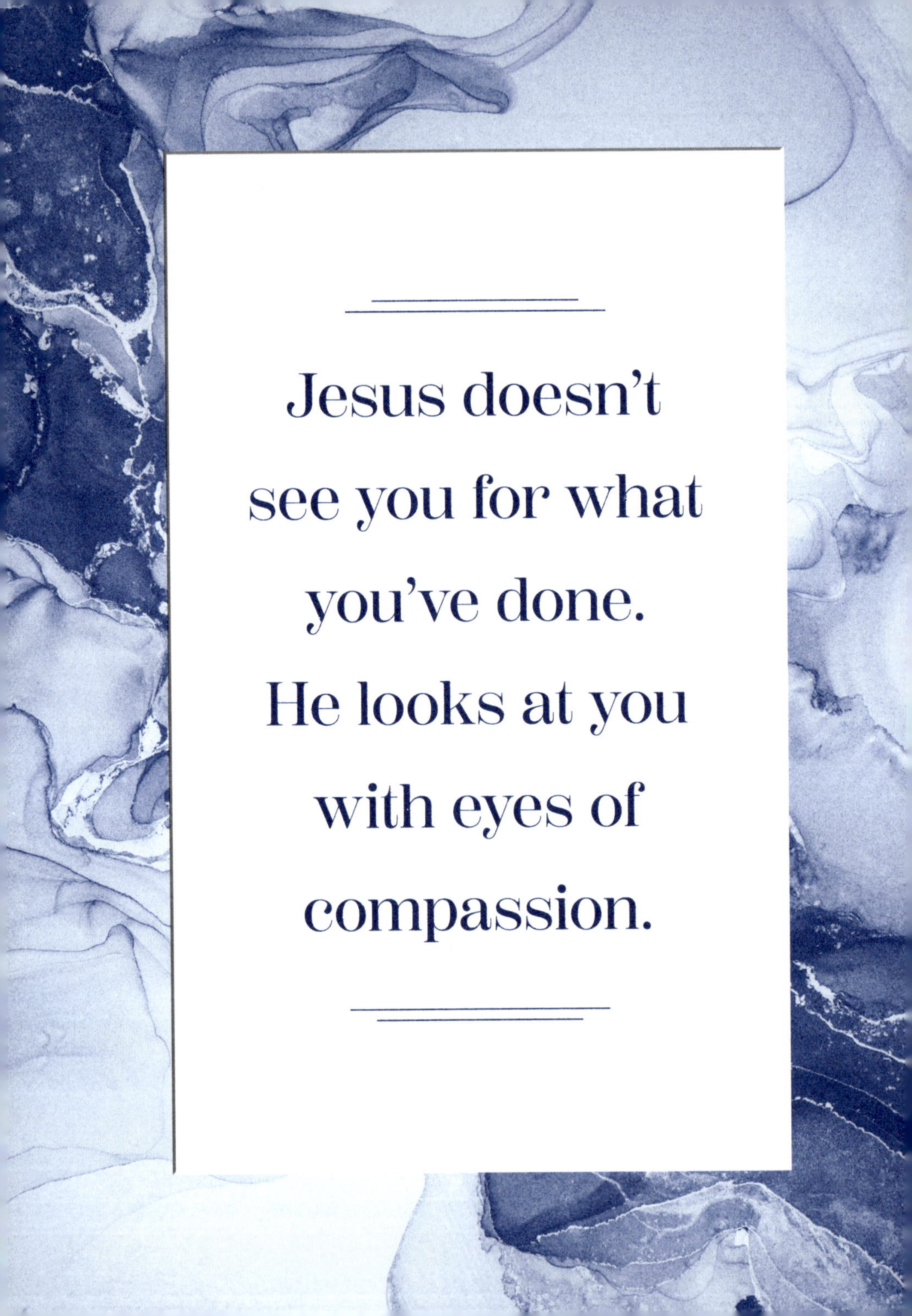
Jesus doesn't
see you for what
you've done.
He looks at you
with eyes of
compassion.

and was now living with a man who wasn't her husband. No wonder she went to the well when she did—everyone in town probably told stories about her.

Christ's kindness and invitation to this Samaritan woman is another beautiful reality of a profound and hopeful truth. Each one of us has personal regrets, and perhaps yours are many and painful. Remember that Christ already knows your story, so you don't need to hide it. Take comfort in the fact that Jesus doesn't see you for what you've done. He looks at you with eyes of compassion, knowing what God's grace can bring about in your life.

The Bible says that many in the town believed in Jesus because of the woman's testimony. Their experience didn't end with her story, though. They then went on to experience Jesus for themselves, and their belief became even deeper (v. 42). Like this transformed woman who went from sketchy past to passionate evangelist, we should seek to be stepping stones for others' faith. When we share with them what Jesus has done in our lives, God can use our stories and testimonies to open hearts to him. We should be faithful witnesses to the love and truth of Christ. Ultimately, however, the work of conversion is God's alone. It's God's Spirit who regenerates hearts to new life in Christ. All we are called to do, like the woman, is to faithfully witness and to leave the rest to Jesus.

DAY 31

Zacchaeus

THE TRANSFORMED TAX COLLECTOR

READ LUKE 19:1–10

Zacchaeus was a wealthy man, and he was also an outcast. This was not because of the size of his bank account, but rather because his wealth was gained from being a tax collector—the "chief tax collector," in fact. As mentioned earlier, tax collectors were hated by the Jews because they took money from their own people on behalf of the Roman government. It didn't help that many of them were also known to charge people too much money, skimming off the extra for themselves. Tax collectors were the predatory lenders (the folks with payday loan operations charging crushing interest rates) of the ancient world. Their wealth came at the expense of their neighbors.

By the time we meet Zacchaeus in Luke's gospel, we are near the end of a long section some have called "the gospel to the outcasts." This section of Luke is a travelogue, documenting Jesus' journey from Galilee to Jerusalem (Luke 9:51; 19:28), where he was ultimately crucified. The intervening text is full of parables and stories illustrating Christ's heart for outsiders and outcasts, and Zacchaeus is the final one. While we usually think of outcasts as the poor or the foreigners, we know Zacchaeus was an outcast for other reasons. Who would want to befriend the chief betrayer of the community? Zacchaeus received no dinner invitations or birthday cards.

Yet something stirred him to want to see Jesus when Christ passed through Jericho. Jesus was often surrounded by throngs of people, which posed a technical challenge to Zacchaeus, who happened to be quite short. He climbed up a sycamore fig tree to cast his eyes over the crowd, hoping to catch a glimpse of Jesus.

We ought to wonder what drew Zacchaeus to Jesus. Quite likely his interest in the Lord had been ignited by stories he'd heard that depicted Jesus as someone who loved outcasts and ignored conventions, someone unafraid to eat with sinners and engage with tax collectors. Perhaps word had reached Zacchaeus that Jesus had even called a tax collector to be one of his disciples! Whatever the case, Zacchaeus was longing for something.

Zacchaeus certainly didn't anticipate what would happen next. Jesus walked straight to the tree he was perched in, looked up, and said, "Zacchaeus, come down immediately. I must stay at your house today" (Luke 19:5). Can you imagine? Jesus, a famed rabbi, wanted to go to the house of the chief tax collector. This man ignored conventions indeed!

While the crowd muttered at Jesus' choice of homes to visit, Zacchaeus professed a new life in Christ. He announced he would give half his possessions to the poor and repay anyone he had cheated four times over. A moment with Jesus transformed his life and softened his heart. Christ affirmed Zacchaeus with powerful words: "Today salvation has come to this house, because this man, too, is a son of Abraham. For the Son of Man came to seek and to save the lost" (vv. 9–10).

Whether you are wealthy in the eyes of others or not, Zacchaeus's story provides a witness to the transforming power of Christ, and to what that transformation should effect in each one of us. When Christ accepts you and you experience the full joy of his grace, your heart and your attitudes will change. You no longer cling to the things of your old life because you've found a new life in Christ. Zacchaeus did what the rich young ruler could not (Mark 10:21–22). He resolved to give his possessions away and turn from his former life.

Your response to God's acceptance of you in Christ may look different from that of Zacchaeus. After all, you are not a first-century tax collector despised by your neighbors for consorting with Rome. Yet, once we find new life in Christ, each one of us should demonstrate repentance

When Christ accepts you and you experience the full joy of his grace, your heart and your attitudes will change.

and show forth the fruit of the Spirit (Galatians 5:22–23). We should become people of generosity, not preoccupied with material wealth but instead ready to give and to serve others out of love for Christ.

Ask yourself today: How has your encounter with Christ changed your life? How has Christ's Spirit adjusted the way you treat others and relate to material wealth? How are you demonstrating the fruit of righteousness and repentance through faithful obedience with your money? The same Christ who welcomed tax collectors welcomes you, and he calls you to live a new life for him.

DAY 32

Thomas

THE RESTORED RATIONALIST

READ JOHN 20:24–29

Faith and doubt have an interesting relationship. At first we might think they're opposites, but that's not quite true. As the book of Hebrews says, faith is "confidence in what we hope for and assurance about what we do not see" (11:1). While "assurance" and "confidence" sound complete, with no room for doubt whatsoever, the fact is that on this side of eternity our faith is always dancing a tango with at least a little bit of doubt. Seasons of doubt will always crop up in life. I have yet to meet a Christian for whom this is not true.

The apostle Thomas is often called "Doubting Thomas" because of his disbelief in the other disciples' testimony that they had seen Christ risen from the dead. While it is easy to disparage Thomas for his doubt, in truth we can hardly blame him. Jesus had died a gruesome death, executed upon a cross. When the other disciples told Thomas they had seen Jesus, he was skeptical.

Thomas's skepticism does seem consistent with the little glimpses of his personality that we get elsewhere in John's gospel. When Jesus told his disciples they were heading to Judea, where the Jewish leaders had obvious hatred and animosity toward Jesus, Thomas responded with what sounds like forlorn resignation: "Let us also go, that we may die with him" (11:16). When Jesus told the disciples he was going to leave them to prepare a place for them, Thomas gave a clinically practical response: "We don't know where you are going, so how can we know the way?" (14:5).

Perhaps Thomas's key trait is not doubt but realism. He took a rational posture to life, which, in the case of Christ's death, manifested itself as skepticism. After all, people don't just come back to life after being executed on a cross. Christ had been speared in the side,

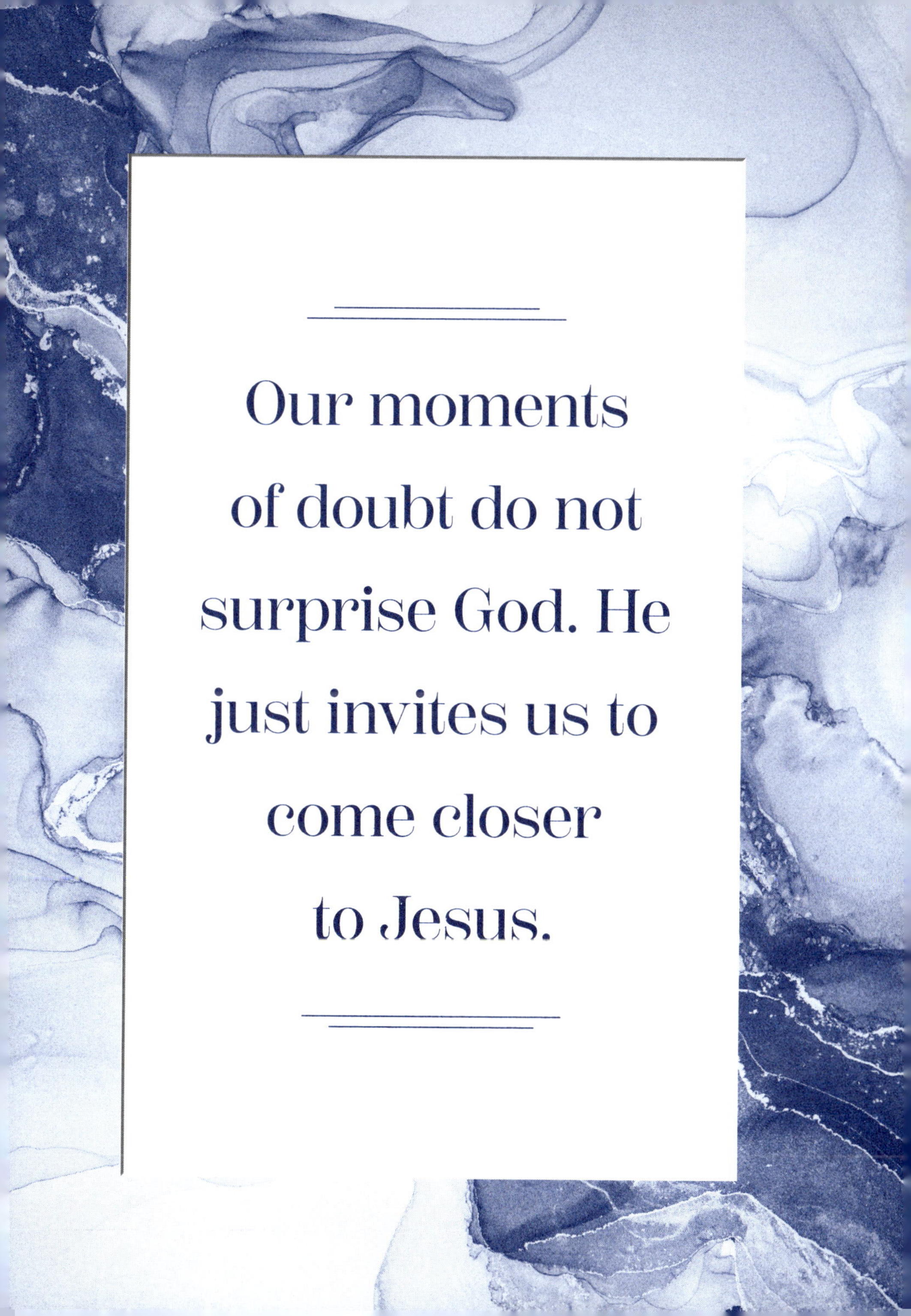
Our moments
of doubt do not
surprise God. He
just invites us to
come closer
to Jesus.

wrapped in grave clothes, and put in a tomb. Wouldn't the rationalists among us think the same thing as Thomas?

Here's the amazing thing: Christ is patient with doubt. In fact, Christ seemed more bothered by fear than by doubt (Matthew 8:26). Perhaps this is because fear keeps people from experiencing the love of God, but doubt can be held by that love. Matthew's account of Christ's resurrection shows that even after Jesus appeared to his disciples, "some doubted" (28:17). So it seems Thomas was not the only one! Yet Jesus did not chastise them. Instead, he drew them to himself.

We see this in the story of Thomas. Christ appeared and offered Thomas the chance to do the exact thing Thomas had named as a requirement for believing Jesus was alive: touch the wounds in Christ's body. When Thomas saw Jesus, however, both his doubt and his faith turned to sight: "My Lord and my God!" (John 20:28). Thomas went from doubting to professing Christ as his Lord and God.

Thomas's experience should be a tremendous comfort. God is patient with our doubts. Doubt does not disqualify us from being children of God. Our moments of doubt do not surprise God. He just invites us to come closer to Jesus. The important thing is not that we are empty of doubt, but that our faith carries us to Jesus despite our doubts. As the hymn by Charlotte Elliott, penned in the 1830s, says: "Just as I am, though tossed about / with many a conflict, many a doubt / fightings and fears within, without / O Lamb of God, I come!"[14] Doubts will come, but the important thing is never to let doubt keep you from moving toward Christ.

The goal is not to live a life free of any doubt. In this life, we'll never fully achieve that. What matters is sharing in the powerful confession of Thomas, coming to Christ, and declaring him to be our Lord and our

God. In our moments of both certainty and struggle, we can rest in his grace. As Jesus promised his first-century followers and still promises us today, “Whoever comes to me I will never drive away” (John 6:37). Though we may yet have seasons of conflict and doubt, we are invited to come to the Lamb of God.

DAY 33

Stephen

THE MIGHTY MARTYR

READ ACTS 7

The first martyr for Christ was Stephen. From the moment Luke (the writer of Acts) introduces Stephen, we're told he's a man of righteous character. Stephen was selected as one of the first deacons of the Christian church, men called upon to help administer food to widows in need. This indicates that Stephen was a man of compassion with a heart for the needy. Acts describes Stephen as being "full of faith and of the Holy Spirit" (6:5) and "full of God's grace and power" (v. 8). God performed wonders and signs through Stephen, which led to opposition from the Jewish religious leaders.

Stephen's opponents tried to argue with him, but their arguments could not stand up to the wisdom God's Spirit granted him in his moment of need (v. 10). Stephen's trial before the Jewish leaders echoes the sham trial of Jesus. His opponents made false accusations against him, saying he blasphemed God and spoke against the law of Moses, and they called upon false witnesses to testify against him. Luke wrote that Stephen's face was like that of an angel during all this.

When asked to give a response, Stephen eloquently delivered one of the most powerful speeches in the Bible. He retold the history of Israel, beginning with Abraham. He accused his accusers of resisting the Holy Spirit and of rejecting and murdering God's righteous one, Jesus Christ. He also accused his opponents of being the ones who rejected God's law.

The Jewish leaders were furious and gnashed their teeth at Stephen. Looking up to heaven, Stephen saw a vision of Christ and told the people he saw the Son of Man standing at the right hand of God. At this, the people dragged Stephen out of the city and stoned him. In a final Christlike moment, Stephen prayed for God to receive his spirit and not to hold the sins of his murderers against them. Then he died.

Stephen's story is one of unshakable faith and trust in God. Even

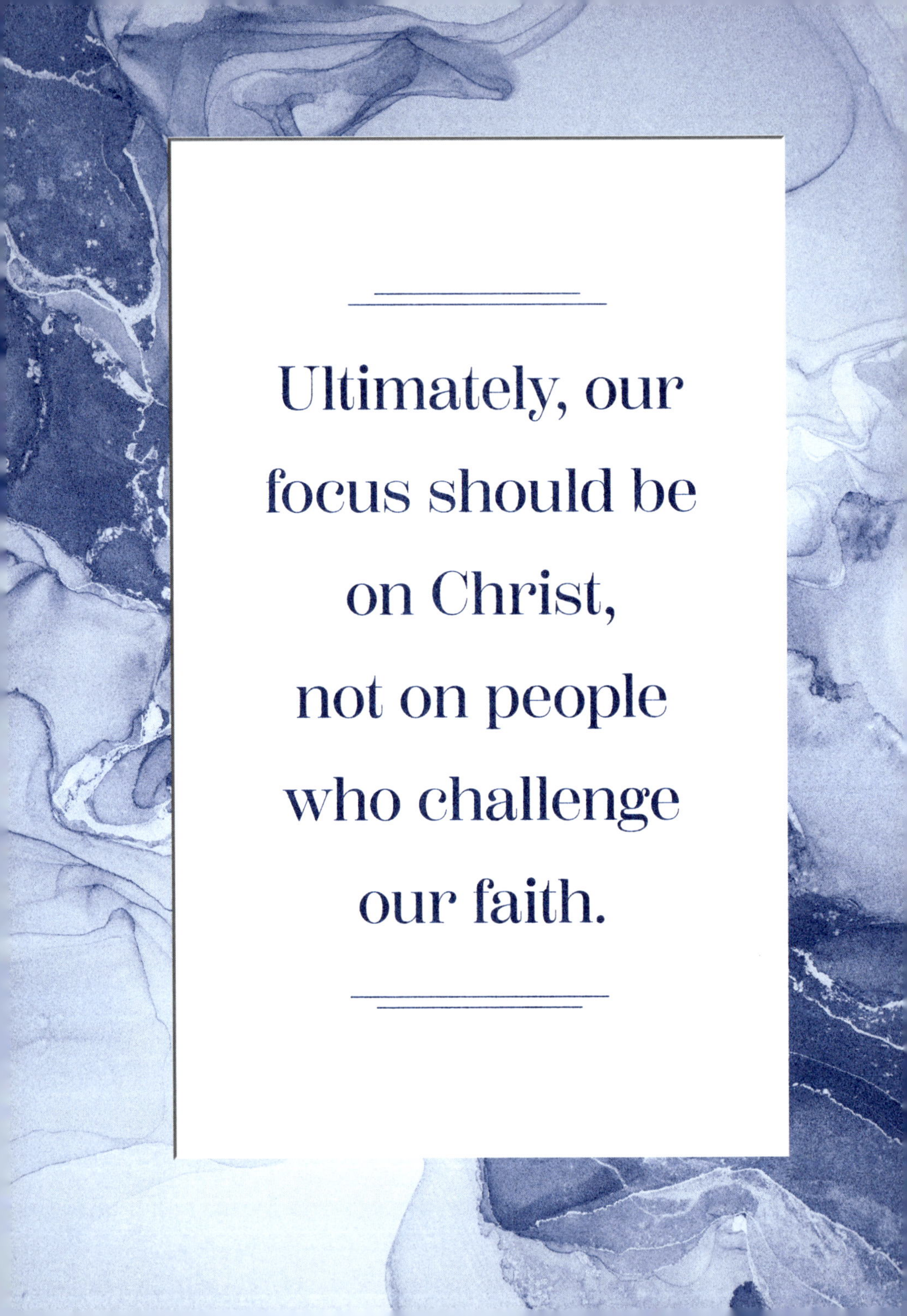
Ultimately, our focus should be on Christ, not on people who challenge our faith.

when it meant certain death, Stephen did not back down from speaking the truth about Christ. This kind of faith should challenge us: How willing are we to boldly stand in our faith against all opposition? Though it may not come to actual violence in our own lives, our faith may draw consternation, judgment, or ridicule from others. How will we react when we experience these things?

The word *martyr* comes from the Greek word meaning "witness." Though most of us will not die for our faith, each follower of Jesus is called to be a witness. We are laborers in God's vineyard, sharing the good news of Christ's death and resurrection. As 1 Peter 3:15 says, we should "always be prepared to give an answer to everyone who asks [us] to give the reason for the hope that [we] have." This means we should always be ready to talk about Jesus.

For many of us, talking about our faith or about Jesus with those who are not believers may be a scary prospect. Remember, God promises to give us wisdom through his Spirit in our time of need. We don't need to try to out-argue people; we just need to testify to our experience with Jesus, like the Samaritan woman and so many others we've read about on this journey.

Ultimately, our focus should be on Christ, not on people who challenge our faith. While Stephen was being wrongfully accused and attacked, he looked to heaven. In our times of struggle, we keep our eyes on Jesus (Hebrews 12:2). Remember, Jesus promises that if we acknowledge him before others, he in turn will acknowledge us before God the Father (Matthew 10:32). Christ is the one who can present us before God "without fault and with great joy" (Jude v. 24). This is the joy 1 Peter 4:13 promises—the joy we await when Christ returns and his glory is revealed. Until then, we are his witnesses.

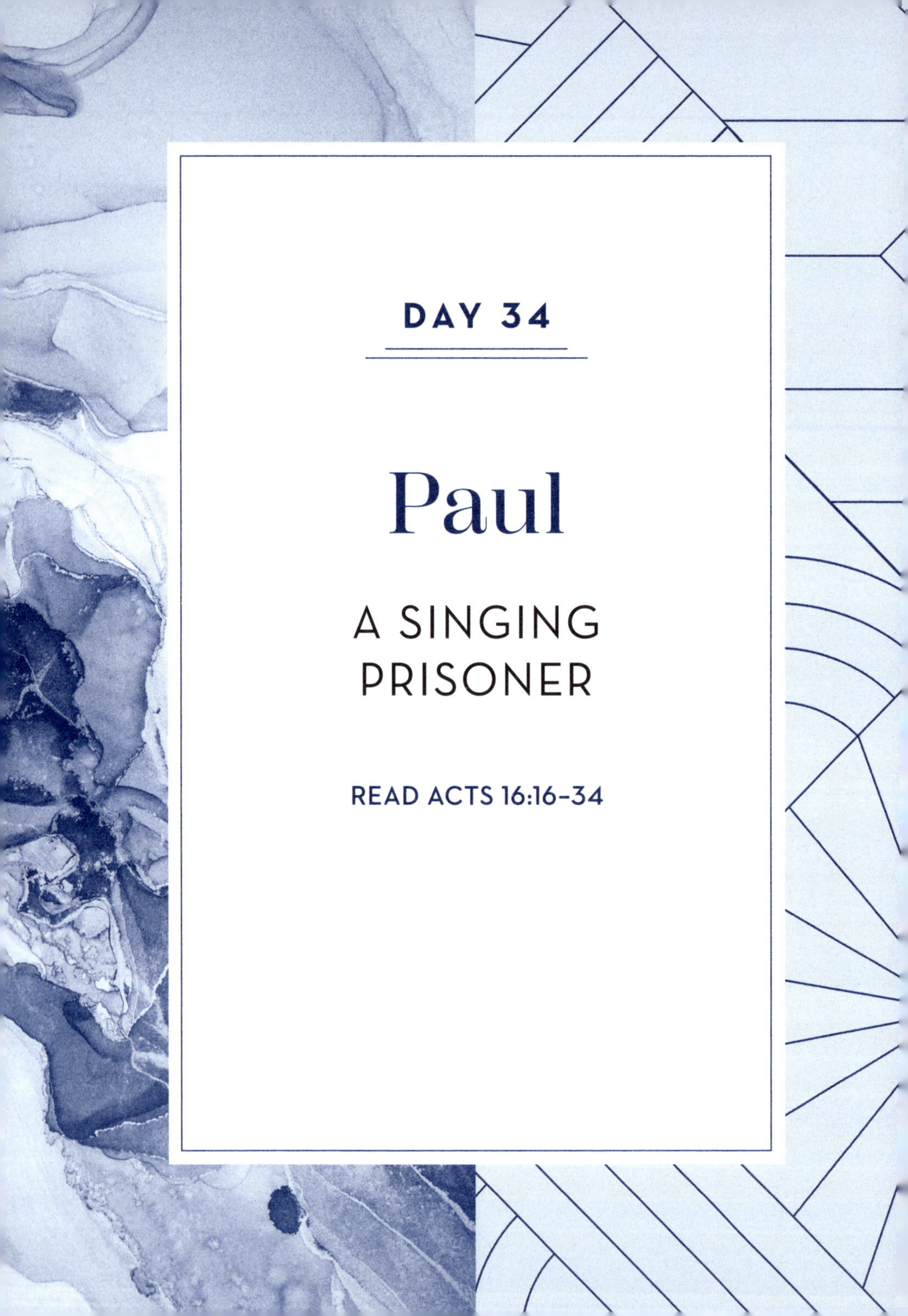

DAY 34

Paul

A SINGING PRISONER

READ ACTS 16:16–34

A butterfly emerging for the first time looks nothing like the caterpillar that built a chrysalis around itself. What was formerly a wormy, trundling leaf eater becomes a majestic, flying, nectar-drinking wonder—truly a "new creation."

In a similar way, Paul wrote that anyone who finds new life in Christ becomes a new creation (2 Corinthians 5:17). He knew this firsthand. Perhaps no person in the Bible displayed this kind of dramatic change more clearly than Paul, and there is perhaps no clearer evidence of his new life than the joy he found in Christ even in the darkest circumstances. Encountering the love of Christ and being regenerated by the Holy Spirit transforms us. We leave behind the old life and enter the new.

Paul went from being a zealous persecutor of the church to a leading missionary, evangelist, and church planter. Once Christ took hold of Paul's life, he never turned back. His entire purpose became glorifying Christ and spreading the gospel. Paul endured numerous trials and hardships because of this. He was imprisoned frequently, flogged severely, pelted with stones multiple times. He endured shipwrecks, hunger, sleep deprivation, and exposure to the elements. Yet he was able to write, "Rejoice in the Lord always. I will say it again: Rejoice! . . . Do not be anxious about anything, but in every situation, by prayer and petition, with thanksgiving, present your requests to God" (Philippians 4:4, 6). Paul was able to find joy even in his sufferings, knowing they would produce perseverance and hope (Romans 5:3–4). Certainly this attitude can only come from a changed spirit—one regenerated by the Holy Spirit!

Acts 16 gives a vivid example of Paul's "rejoice in all situations" attitude. In Philippi, Paul encountered a female slave who had a spirit that enabled her to tell the future. Paul cast the spirit out of the woman, which made her owners furious—her fortune-telling had been a lucrative source of income for them. They stirred up a riot against Paul and Silas, who were stripped and beaten and then locked up in the inner cell of a prison with their feet bound in stocks.

How would you feel if you were Paul? You had done a good thing, delivering a woman from an oppressive spirit. But then you'd been stripped, beaten, and imprisoned without trial. Most of us would probably feel bitter, or at least deeply discouraged. But what did Paul and Silas do in that inner prison cell? They started praying and singing hymns to God. This certainly grabbed the attention of the other prisoners!

When an earthquake shook the prison doors open, and the prisoners were set free, the prison guard panicked. He thought the prisoners had surely escaped and that he would pay for it with his life. Paul assured him, however, that none of the prisoners had left. In a moment of conversion that can only be attributed to God's Spirit, the guard fell before Paul and Silas and asked, "What must I do to be saved?" (16:30). Far from being bitter toward their captor, they encouraged the guard to believe in the Lord Jesus Christ. They shared the word of Christ with him and those in his household, and all of them were baptized. Their newfound faith filled them with the joy of Christ (vv. 33–34).

How can you give praise to God even in your bleakest moments, like Paul and Silas? It can only come from one place: a new identity in Christ. In Christ you learn to die to the old self and begin a new life in which you don't think only of yourself. You begin to learn what it means for your whole mindset to be fixed on Jesus. When you learn this lesson, even suffering can't sway you. Hardships become opportunities to identify with Christ in his own suffering.

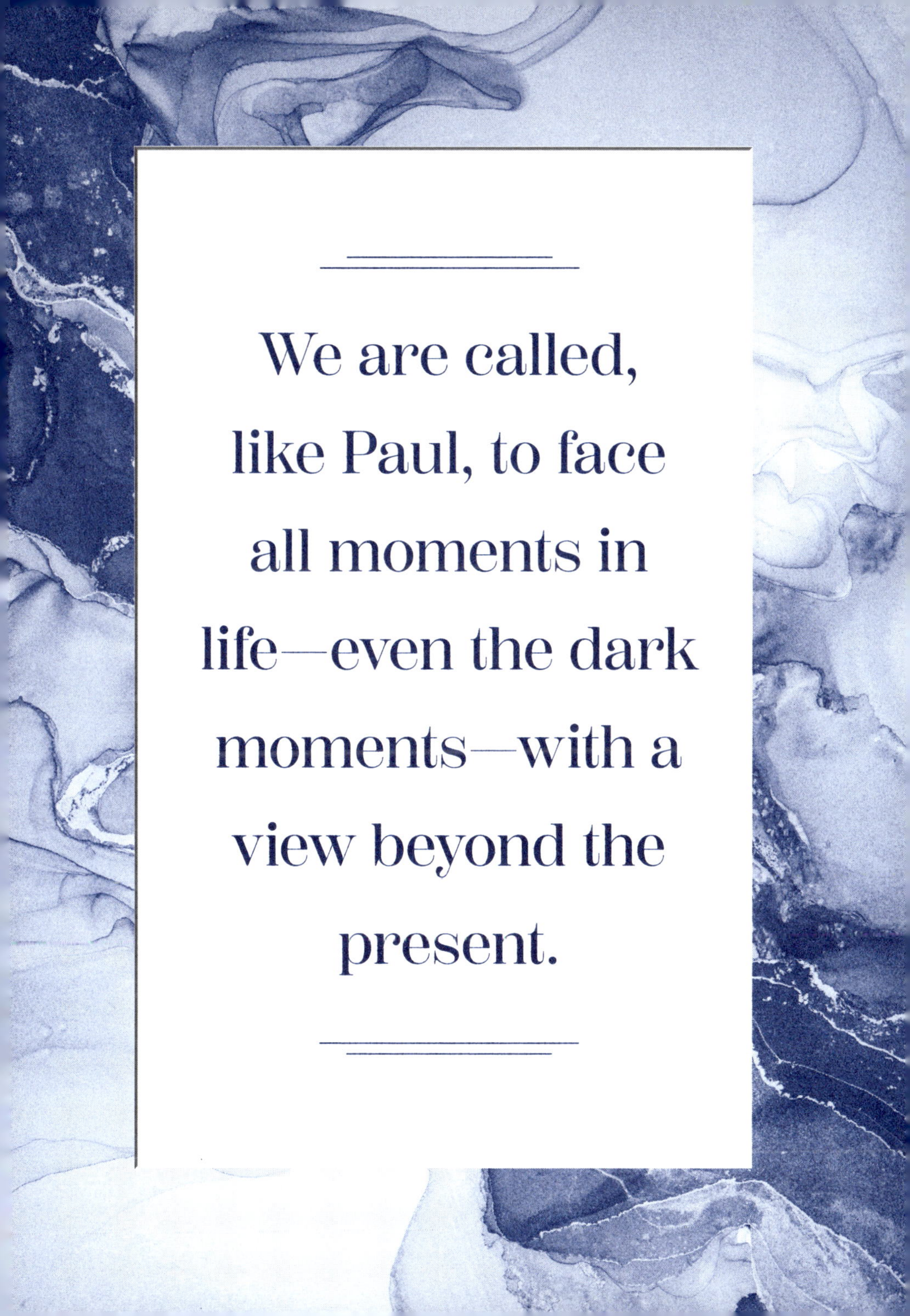
We are called,
like Paul, to face
all moments in
life—even the dark
moments—with a
view beyond the
present.

We are called, like Paul, to face all moments in life—even the dark moments—with a view beyond the present. As Paul wrote, "Our light and momentary troubles are achieving for us an eternal glory that far outweighs them all" (2 Corinthians 4:17). This does not mean dismissing the sufferings of our lives. But God's glorious future can provide a different outlook than what is right now.

Paul's ability to praise God even through sufferings should be an encouragement to every believer to expand our vision beyond the present. Our hope is not that God will deliver us from every trial. God does not show himself good because he prevents bad things from happening to us. Christians and non-Christians alike will experience suffering and sorrow. Instead, God shows himself good because he is with us even in our darkest moments, working even the worst we experience for good in the kingdom of Christ.

DAY 35

Barnabas

A GREAT ENCOURAGER

READ ACTS 9:26–31

Can you remember a time when someone encouraged you or affirmed your giftedness in a certain area? I can still remember when I was in second grade and my art teacher complimented the picture of a peregrine falcon I drew. No, I haven't gone on to be a great artist, but at the time his encouragement meant a lot to me. Perhaps you have pursued a particular career or area of study based on the encouragement someone gave you early on. A good encourager can make a world of difference.

In Acts 4:36–37, Luke introduced us to a man named Joseph, who the apostles called Barnabas, which means "son of encouragement." Barnabas, a Levite by background, sold a field he owned and gave the money to the apostles for the Christian community. Barnabas had an important role in the book of Acts as a ministry partner for the apostle Paul.

Christ transformed Paul's life through a dramatic encounter on the road to Damascus (Acts 9:1–19). Paul received the Holy Spirit and was baptized, and he began preaching the word of Christ in the synagogues. When Paul went to Jerusalem and tried to join the other disciples of Christ, however, they were afraid of him. It was Barnabas who took Paul under his wing and advocated for him with the disciples. Barnabas told the believers the story of Paul's conversion and the way Paul had preached fearlessly in the name of Jesus. At Barnabas's testimony, the disciples accepted Paul, who went on to become the greatest evangelist of the early church. It took Barnabas's trust and encouragement to bring these two parties together.

Paul and Barnabas went on to minister together. When the believers in Jerusalem heard that Gentiles in Antioch were turning to Christ, they sent Barnabas to see them. Barnabas encouraged them "to remain

Christianity is not a "lone wolf" religion. We need the support and encouragement of others, and we need to offer support and encouragement as well.

true to the Lord with all their hearts" (Acts 11:23), and many more people came to the Lord. Barnabas then found Paul and brought him to Antioch, where the two ministered and taught about Jesus for an entire year. They went on to do more missionary work, preaching boldly and performing signs and wonders (14:3) as they moved from one place to another. As they traveled through various cities, they appointed elders over each church. Barnabas knew the importance of godly leaders to guide and encourage a faith community.

Barnabas was certainly a powerful person in the early church, and his story offers encouragement to us today. Barnabas was willing to sell his own property to support the ministry of Christ's church. He preached boldly for Christ everywhere he went, even in the face of hard opposition. Most importantly, Barnabas was an encourager. He had a heart for building up others in the faith. As you think about the story of Barnabas, reflect on who God has used in your life to encourage and nurture your own faith. It may have been a grandparent, a teacher, a pastor, or simply a Christian friend. God puts these people in our lives for a reason. Their encouragement spurs us deeper in our own faith.

But don't just thank God for the encouragers he has placed on your path. Take time today to consider who God has placed in your life for you to encourage. Are there people who are not as far along on their faith journey as you are? Are there people working in ministry who could use some encouragement? Perhaps you could show your love and support for the ministry volunteers or leaders in your church, writing them a note to let them know you are praying for them. Perhaps you could serve as a mentor, either formally or casually, for a younger believer.

Christianity is not a "lone wolf" religion. We need the support and encouragement of others, and we need to offer support and encouragement as well. As Paul wrote, we rejoice with those who rejoice and we mourn with those who mourn (Romans 12:15). We need one another. Don't stand on the sidelines. Offer your enthusiasm, gifts, and encouragement to others "so that the body of Christ might be built up" (Ephesians 4:12).

Priscilla and Aquila

A MENTORING COUPLE

READ ACTS 18:18–28

In Acts 18, we're introduced to a married couple named Priscilla and Aquila. Paul met them in Corinth, where he lived and ministered for a year and a half. Priscilla and Aquila had previously resided in Rome, but they had been displaced when the emperor Claudius ordered all the Jews to leave the city. Paul stayed with them, and since they shared the same tent-making trade, Paul and Aquila also worked together. We can only imagine that Paul and this couple had countless conversations about Christ and the gospel during the many months they spent together in Corinth.

Aquila and Priscilla eventually moved to Ephesus, while Paul continued to travel. There, they heard a man named Apollos preaching about Jesus. Apollos was a Jew from Alexandria, Egypt. He was a gifted speaker, knowledgeable in the Scriptures, and a believer. However, Luke wrote that Apollos "knew only the baptism of John" (Acts 18:25). Gifted and passionate though he was, he still lacked some understanding about the Holy Spirit and the gospel.

Luke wrote, "When Priscilla and Aquila heard him, they invited him to their home and explained to him the way of God more adequately" (v. 26). Apparently strengthened by their guidance and mentoring, Apollos went on from there to continue teaching about Jesus, "proving from the Scriptures that Jesus was the Messiah" (v. 28). Hearing him teach in the synagogue, Aquila and Priscilla discerned God calling them to mentor Apollos in his knowledge of the faith.

Did Priscilla and Aquila invite him to stay with them for a little while, or was it just a short meeting? We cannot know how long the mentoring partnership between this couple and Apollos lasted. What is certain is that this husband and wife took hold of an opportunity to assist an aspiring and gifted preacher and evangelist.

When we hear someone say something we don't think is theologically quite right, it's easy to dismiss that person as not a true believer. Aquila and Priscilla show us a better way: Invite the person over and encourage them! While this might not always be possible or appropriate, it is surely a more Christlike response.

It is common to see new, passionate Christ followers like Apollos burn out in their faith. While we can hold out hope that God will continue to work in their lives, it's possible their fizzled-out faith is a result of a lack of meaningful mentorship and accountability in their lives. They get excited about Jesus, but when discouragement or trials come, they give up because their faith hasn't had time to mature. They are like the seed planted in rocky soil; the plant springs up quickly but fades away when trouble comes because it has no root (Matthew 13:20–21). God uses good mentors to help the seed of the gospel take root in good soil in our lives.

It's also important to note that in mentorship, we must be humble and not presumptuous. We should be patient with the person we are seeking to help, praying for God's abundant blessing upon their life and ministry. As Isaiah said, "A bruised reed he will not break, and a smoldering wick he will not snuff out" (42:3). Matthew 12:20 applies this verse to Jesus, and like Jesus, we should be sensitive and nurturing of the faith of others. Good mentoring requires patience and encouragement.

Mentoring opportunities can take all sorts of forms, from formal to casual. Perhaps there is a local school with a mentoring program you could volunteer for, giving attention and care to a young person who needs a positive influence in their life. Perhaps you can simply offer support and encouragement for people you know who are new to the faith.

God uses good mentors to help the seed of the gospel take root in good soil in our lives.

Maybe there is a church program you can be part of where you can share your faith and heart for Jesus with others.

I still think fondly of the mentoring relationship I had in seminary. I know firsthand the important role that a relationship like this can have in developing one's faith and gifts for God's kingdom. As you read about Aquila and Priscilla, ask yourself two questions: First, do you need a mentor in your life? Don't try to live out your faith alone. Seek out someone you trust, even for something as simple as going out for coffee once a month to talk about faith and life. Second, consider who God has put in your life who you could serve as a mentor for. You have your own unique story and life experiences. Your journey with Jesus can bless and encourage someone else. Don't underestimate what God is able to do through you when you seek ways to bless and nurture the faith of those around you.

DAY 37

Lydia

A WEALTHY WITNESS

READ ACTS 16:11–15

Wealth and faith often seem to have a complicated relationship. The Bible says that "the love of money is a root of all kinds of evil" and that desire for money has led some to wander from the faith (1 Timothy 6:10). In his explanation of the parable of the sower, Jesus said that the deceitfulness of wealth can choke out the Word in a person's life and make it unfruitful. When a certain rich young man came to Jesus asking about eternal life, Jesus told him, "Go, sell everything you have and give to the poor" (Mark 10:21). At the same time, the book of Proverbs praises proper use of wealth, extolling the virtue of saving and building wealth for the future (13:22). Jesus' ministry was supported financially by women of means (Luke 8:3).

It seems, then, that the problem is not with wealth itself but with our relationship to it (1 Timothy 6:17). The question to ask is: Are we using our wealth and resources for God's kingdom? Lydia's story, in Acts 16, provides a biblical example of what this looks like.

In Macedonia Paul and his companions came to the city of Philippi, a prominent Roman outpost. It appears there was no synagogue in Philippi, because instead of starting his evangelism there like usual, Paul found a "place of prayer" by the river outside the city (v. 13). The people who were gathered for prayer were women from the city. Paul's company sat and shared the message of Jesus with them.

One of the women was Lydia, a merchant who dealt in purple cloth. The Lord opened her heart to receive the gospel of Christ, and she and her household were baptized. Lydia invited Paul and his companions to stay in her home. The fact that she was a merchant of royal cloth and is described as having a household suggests she was a woman of considerable means.

It's likely that the church in Philippi met together at Lydia's home

The question to ask is: Are we using our wealth and resources for God's kingdom?

(v. 40). In Paul's letter to the Philippians, written from captivity, Paul thanked them for sending money to support him: "Not one church shared with me in the matter of giving and receiving, except you only; for even when I was in Thessalonica, you sent me aid more than once when I was in need" (4:15–16). Paul did not name Lydia specifically in this word of gratitude, but it is safe to imagine that, being a woman of considerable means, she was a key part of this ongoing financial support.

Lydia's conversion to Christ marked an inflection point in the growth of the church. She was the first European convert named in the Bible. Her story shows that having wealth is not itself a bad thing. God blessed Lydia with success, and she was generous with what she had.

Every Christmas season people demonstrate similar generosity by choosing an "angel"—a child or older person who they can then choose a gift for—off an angel tree. This is a special part of the holiday for the givers and for those on the receiving end. During the rest of the year, churches often help people who need a hand up, sustaining them during their hour of need.

What resources has God blessed you with? How can you use whatever you've been given for God's kingdom? Consider practical ways you can support ministries and missions that work for righteousness and justice, whether locally or far away. This is not an onerous tax on what's "yours"; instead, it's a joyful act of participation in the shared kingdom work we've been given. Remember, every good and perfect gift comes from God, and those gifts should be used for his glory.

We each have different capacities to give based on our resources. Jesus said the widow who offered two copper coins gave more to the treasury than wealthy people who put in large sums (Mark 12:41–44). The amount is not the important thing. Our mindset is what counts.

DAY 38

Cornelius

A SURPRISING CHURCH MEMBER

READ ACTS 10

Earlier on this journey, we read about Hezekiah, a king of Jerusalem who led the nation in renewal and revival. Part of his religious reforms included an enormous Passover celebration, such as Israel had never experienced before. Remarkably, this Passover celebration broke several "rules." For one thing, they celebrated the Passover in the wrong month for logistical reasons. More striking, Hezekiah allowed people to celebrate the Passover who were not clean according to the law. These people, from the Northern Kingdom of Israel, "ate the Passover, contrary to what was written. But Hezekiah prayed for them, saying, 'May the Lord, who is good, pardon everyone who sets their heart on seeking God—the Lord, the God of their ancestors—even if they are not clean according to the rules of the sanctuary.' And the Lord heard Hezekiah and healed the people" (2 Chronicles 30:18–20). God widened the invitation!

In the book of Acts, we see God open the invitation to membership in the church in a way Christ's first disciples never anticipated. They thought that people needed to be or become Jews in order to follow Christ. Through Cornelius, however, God showed Peter this was not the case. The invitation was wider than any had imagined.

Cornelius was a centurion, a devout and God-fearing man. Cornelius was also generous, known for helping the needy. One day God's angel came to Cornelius in a vision. The angel commended Cornelius for his faithful prayers and for his generosity to the poor. Then the angel told him to send for the disciple Peter. Cornelius obeyed.

Peter himself received a vision from God around the same time. In it he saw a sheet suspended from the air, filled with animals of every kind. A voice told Peter to get up and eat, but Peter refused, saying, "Surely not, Lord! . . . I have never eaten anything impure or unclean." The voice responded, "Do not call anything impure that God has made clean" (Acts 10:14–15).

The messengers from Cornelius found Peter, and the next day he set out with them. When they came to Cornelius's house, Peter had a choice to make. As a Jew, it would have been against the rules for him to enter the house of a Gentile. Doing so would have made him ritually unclean. At the same time, the vision God had given him was germinating in his heart. Peter entered the house.

Cornelius fell at Peter's feet, but Peter told him to rise. Then Peter and Cornelius shared with each other the messages they had both received from God. Cornelius said, "We are all here in the presence of God to listen to everything the Lord has commanded you to tell us" (v. 33). His heart was longing to hear God's truth.

Peter shared the story of Jesus with Cornelius and his household, testifying also to the way his own eyes were being opened to the new thing God was doing: "I now realize how true it is that God does not show favoritism but accepts from every nation the one who fears him and does what is right" (vv. 34–35). When Peter shared the message of Christ with his Gentile listeners, the Holy Spirit came upon them. Seeing the power of the Holy Spirit upon the Gentiles, Peter declared they should also be baptized. This was a second Pentecost, one in which God widened the invitation into his community.

Cornelius's story shows us the beauty of the wideness of God's love. As we have seen many times on this journey, God's grace is surprising. God calls people we might not expect to be his powerful and devoted servants. We should be ready for God to do the same thing today. We cannot put boundaries on God's love. God doesn't judge by externals like race, nationality, or status. God looks at the heart.

He sends his Spirit to gather children from every language and nation (Revelation 7:9).

Those of us who are Gentiles should rejoice in the story of Cornelius. We are heirs of the same surprising grace. We were outsiders, brought in by the mercy of God. As Paul wrote to Gentile readers, “But now in Christ Jesus you who once were far away have been brought near by the blood of Christ” (Ephesians 2:13). The fact that we were outsiders brought in by grace should instill in us the same compassionate spirit Cornelius had, praying for and serving those who are still outsiders. God calls us to widen the invitation, to go out and bring even the most surprising and unlikely people in (Luke 14:15–24). Praise God for the broadness of his grace!

We cannot put boundaries on God's love. God doesn't judge by externals like race, nationality, or status. God looks at the heart.

DAY 39

Timothy

A FAITHFUL YOUNG MAN

READ 2 TIMOTHY 1:5

Everyone has a different testimony about coming to faith. Some had dramatic conversions where they were rescued from lives of substance abuse or criminal habits before becoming passionate followers of Jesus. Others grew up in Christian homes, always went to church, and have been believers ever since. If the latter is your story, consider that it is not a "boring" testimony; it is actually beautiful too.

I wonder if Timothy sometimes felt like his story wasn't very interesting, especially when he was traveling around doing missionary work with Paul. Paul, of course, had a dramatic conversion story, from persecutor of the church to servant of Christ. Paul's testimony must have held people's attention every time he told it. We might imagine that Paul would then look over at young Timothy and invite him forward: "And now tell everyone *your* story, Timothy!"

Timothy's story wasn't dramatic. He had been raised in the faith by his grandmother Lois and his mother, Eunice. When Paul encountered Timothy and told him about Christ, it was a natural extension of the faith in God Timothy already had. His life didn't have the dramatic turn that Paul's did.

But Timothy's story is beautiful. Being raised in a Christian home, taught about God's love through Christ Jesus from an early age, is a tremendous gift. Sometimes in churches we valorize the dramatic conversion story: from abject rebellious sin to vibrant servant of Jesus. Of course those stories are remarkable, but God's grace for people like Timothy is just as amazing. Perhaps you have a story more like Timothy's. Give God praise for that!

Timothy's faith made him an energetic ministry partner for Paul. He joined Paul in his missionary work. He was also sent by Paul to check on how certain churches were doing, bringing word back of the faith of believers in other areas (1 Thessalonians 3:1–10; 1 Corinthians 4:17; Philippians 2:19). He became the pastor of the church at Ephesus. Paul told Timothy not to let anyone look down on him because he was young, but to instead set an example for all believers through his speech, conduct, love, faith, and purity (1 Timothy 4:12).

We can find Timothy's story tremendously encouraging, chiefly because it is not dramatic. You may never have been scooped by God from the depths of rebellion. But Timothy showed us that all believers bear witness to God's grace in powerful ways. The important thing is that we direct our lives toward God and use the gifts that he has given us for his purposes.

Think about your own story of coming to faith and give thanks to God for the way he led you to himself, whether it is full of twists and turns or if you embraced the Christian faith from a young age. Praise God for the people who taught you about Christ and modeled his grace. Look for ways to be a model of faith and an encouragement in the faith of others. Don't feel like you don't have a story to tell. God can use your testimony to bless and strengthen others.

God brings all kinds of people into his community, and each one is uniquely equipped to reach out to other people with similar experiences, interests, or personalities. Who knows whom God might intend to build up through your faithful witness and willingness to share about Christ?

Don't feel like you don't have a story to tell. God can use your testimony to bless and strengthen others.

John

A VISION OF HOPE

READ REVELATION 1

Charles Dickens's classic novel *A Christmas Carol* has been made into countless films and parodies, many of which are rebroadcast every Christmas season. The story centers on a curmudgeonly miser named Ebenezer Scrooge, a wealthy man without an ounce of generosity or love. Scrooge is visited by three spirits: the Ghost of Christmas Past, the Ghost of Christmas Present, and the Ghost of Christmas Yet to Come. The final spirit reveals to Scrooge that his selfish life is headed for a sad, lonely, and fatal end. Seeing the reality of the future, Ebenezer Scrooge disavows himself of his unloving ways to become a person of generosity and compassion. Having seen the future, Scrooge changes his behavior in the present.

The book of Revelation is similar. God gave John this revelation from Jesus Christ "to show his servants what must soon take place" (1:1). God pulled back the curtain to show his people the future, and John's vision of the future victory of Christ encourages and strengthens believers to live faithful lives today.

John was one of Jesus' closest disciples. When Jesus split off from the larger group, he often brought John with him, along with Peter and James. When Jesus was hanging on the cross, he entrusted his mother into the care of John (John 19:27). John is credited with writing the gospel that bears his name, three eponymous epistles, and the book of Revelation.

By the time John wrote Revelation, he was an old man. John knew suffering and patient endurance all too well, and so did many of the other Christians. Some were certainly beginning to lose heart: When would Jesus return? Why hadn't he returned already? How could God allow the persecution of his followers under Roman emperors such as Nero and Domitian? John addressed this problem by showing them the future: a glorious vision graciously given to him by God.

At Christ's command, John wrote down his vision of the present and the future for the seven churches (Revelation 1:19). This vision is not for those churches alone, however; it is for all believers since to read and find encouragement through. While the book of Revelation has been subject to endless debate and interpretive disagreements throughout church history, the broad contours are clear. Christ will be victorious in the end. He will return and establish a new heaven and a new earth. He will reign with his people in a glorious kingdom in which there will be no more death or pain. God's faithful children can rejoice in the sure promise of this glorious future, guaranteed by the precious blood of our Savior, Jesus Christ.

Most of us are not facing the same kind of persecution today. Nevertheless, we feel these same questions nagging at our minds. *Why hasn't Jesus returned yet? Why does God allow such suffering and strife to continue?* John understood the weariness of waiting. He had seen or heard about many other Christians—even his fellow apostles—being martyred for their faith. Yet John maintained his zeal and passion for Christ to the end. John showed us what a long and faithful obedience looks like.

In these moments, the book of Revelation is a comfort. We can remind ourselves that God's patience is a facet of his grace, giving time for the gospel to spread and for more people to come to life in Christ. When we feel the weight of a hurting world around us and wonder why God lets it go on, we can look to John's vision as deeply moving and comforting. Beyond the chaos of today and beyond the chaos to come, Christ will prevail as Lord over the universe.

Seeing and believing this future gives us strength to face the moments and days before us, difficult as they may be. Those who are

Beyond the chaos of today and beyond the chaos to come, Christ will prevail as Lord over the universe.

growing old and may be weary in their faith can look to this vision and be renewed. As the prophet Habakkuk also saw, "The revelation awaits an appointed time; it speaks of the end and will not prove false. Though it linger, wait for it; it will certainly come and will not delay" (2:3).

The same is true of John's God-given vision of the future. We wait for it to arrive. Our hope in the coming Lord carries us through the chaos and uncertainty of today. Like John, may each of us remain faithful as we await the day when "every eye will see him" (Revelation 1:7). As our Lord promises, "Look, I am coming soon! Blessed is the one who keeps the words of the prophecy written in this scroll" (22:7).

Amen. Come, Lord Jesus—and find us faithful to the end!

Notes

1. Department of Ancient Near Eastern Art, "Early Dynastic Sculpture, 2900–2350 B.C.," Metropolitan Museum of Art, October 2004, https://www.metmuseum.org/toah/hd/edys/hd_edys.htm.
2. John Walton, "Proposition 7" and "Proposition 8" in *The Lost World of Genesis One: Ancient Cosmology and the Origins Debate* (InterVarsity Press, 2009).
3. Saul McLeod, PhD, "Solomon Asch Conformity Line Experiment Study," Simply Psychology, October 24, 2023, https://www.simplypsychology.org/asch-conformity.html.
4. Ronald W. Richardson, *Becoming a Healthier Pastor: Family Systems Theory and the Pastor's Own Family* (Fortress Press, 2005), 17.
5. Byron Howard, Jared Bush, and Charise Castro Smith, directors, *Encanto* (Walt Disney Animation Studios, 2021), streaming.
6. C. S. Lewis, *The Voyage of the Dawn Treader* (HarperCollins, 1994), 113–16.
7. "The Sierpinski Triangle," Mathigon, accessed April 28, 2025, https://mathigon.org/course/fractals/sierpinski#:~:text

=The%20Sierpinski%20triangle%20is%20a,1969)%20was%20a%20Polish%20mathematician.

8. Laurent Bouzereau, director, *Music by John Williams* (Imagine Documentaries, 2024), streaming.
9. Sidney Lumet, director, *12 Angry Men* (Orion-Nova Productions, 1957), streaming.
10. Ira Spar, "Sennacherib and Jerusalem," The MET, November 24, 2014, https://www.metmuseum.org/exhibitions/listings/2014/assyria-to-iberia/blog/posts/sennacherib-and-jerusalem.
11. William Green, *Richer, Wiser, Happier: How the World's Greatest Investors Win in Markets and Life* (Scribner, 2021), 243–47.
12. George Frideric Handel et al., *Messiah* (1743), monographic.
13. C. S. Lewis, *Mere Christianity* (Macmillan, 1952), 40–41.
14. Charlotte Elliott, "Just As I Am," *Hours of Sorrow Cheered and Comforted* (1836).

THE NIV APPLICATION COMMENTARY SERIES

Old Testament Volumes

Genesis, John H. Walton

Exodus, Peter Enns

Leviticus, Numbers, Roy Gane

Deuteronomy, Daniel I. Block

Joshua, Robert L. Hubbard Jr.

Judges, Ruth, K. Lawson Younger Jr.

1 and 2 Samuel, Bill T. Arnold

1 and 2 Kings, August H. Konkel

1 and 2 Chronicles, Andrew E. Hill

Ezra-Nehemiah, Donna Petter and Thomas Petter

Esther, Karen H. Jobes

Job, John H. Walton

Psalms Volume 1, Gerald H. Wilson

Psalms Volume 2, W. Dennis Tucker Jr. and Jamie A. Grant

Proverbs, Paul E. Koptak

Ecclesiastes, Song of Songs, Iain Provan

Isaiah, John N. Oswalt

Jeremiah, Lamentations, J. Andrew Dearman

Ezekiel, Iain M. Duguid

Daniel, Tremper Longman III

Hosea, Amos, Micah, Gary V. Smith

Jonah, Nahum, Habakkuk, Zephaniah, James Bruckner

Joel, Obadiah, Malachi, David W. Baker

Haggai, Zechariah, Mark J. Boda

New Testament Volumes

Matthew, Michael J. Wilkins

Mark, David E. Garland

Luke, Darrell L. Bock

John, Gary M. Burge

Acts, Ajith Fernando

Romans, Douglas J. Moo

1 Corinthians, Craig L. Blomberg

2 Corinthians, Scott J. Hafemann

Galatians, Scot McKnight

Ephesians, Klyne Snodgrass

Philippians, Frank Thielman

Colossians, Philemon, David E. Garland

1 and 2 Thessalonians, Michael W. Holmes

1 and 2 Timothy, Titus, Walter L. Liefeld

Hebrews, George H. Guthrie

James, David P. Nystrom

1 Peter, Scot McKnight

2 Peter, Jude, Douglas J. Moo

Letters of John, Gary M. Burge

Revelation, Craig S. Keener

NIV APPLICATION BIBLE

Learn what the Bible means.
Discover what it means for you.

Featuring thousands of study notes drawn from the bestselling NIV Application Commentary series, the *NIV Application Bible* helps you understand Scripture and connect it to your world in a whole new way. This study Bible guides you in discovering how the ancient truths found in Scripture relate to your experiences today using insight from trusted evangelical scholars, paired with timely biblical application principles.

Throughout the Bible, **Original Meaning Notes** help you understand the meaning of each passage in its context while **Application Notes** make it personal, helping you to integrate the Bible's teachings into everyday life.

The *NIV Application Bible* pairs a deeper understanding of the ancient biblical text with contemporary application of the lessons found within it, offering you a new way to understand what the Word of God means for your world today.

Features:

- **Complete text** of the accurate, readable, and clear New International Version (NIV)
- **Book Introductions** provide perspective and application for every book of the Bible, plus timelines, reading guides, and more.
- **People to Know articles** show the good and bad of Bible characters' lives, how God accomplished his purposes through them, and lessons we can learn from them about living a faithful life.
- **Character of God articles** explore aspects of God's character and what these mean for our lives as believers.
- **Questions for Growth** in each chapter of the Bible encourage reflection.

The *NIV Application Bible* includes full-color maps, reading plans, an NIV dictionary-concordance, and words of Jesus in red. Available in multiple formats and sizes, including hardcover, bonded leather, leathersoft, personal size, and large print.

Enjoy an excerpt from the Mark Bible Study

ISBN 978-0-310-18185-9

Mark wrote his account of the life and ministry of Jesus during the time that first-century Christians were facing intense persecution because of their faith. Just like Mark's readers, you need to know that your faith is built on a solid foundation. In this twelve-lesson study, you will explore the context of Mark's Gospel and examine what you can glean from what he wrote and—just as importantly—what he didn't write. This is an invitation for you to learn more about Jesus and life in his kingdom as you examine this unique Gospel from the perspectives of a first-century Christian *and* a twenty-first-century Christian.

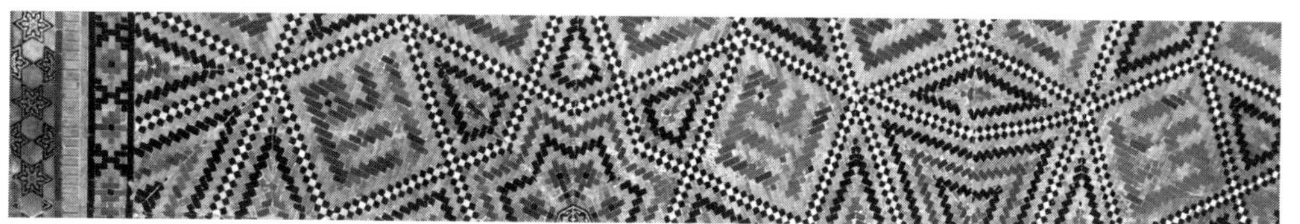

About the
BIBLE STUDY SERIES

Life transformation ... that is the bottom line. When the Holy Spirit spoke through James and said that followers of Christ are not to "merely listen to the word" but actually "do what it says" (1:22), it was a declaration that academic study of the Bible is not the whole story. God desires for us to read the Bible, seek to understand it in both its *original* context and in *today's* culture, and then allow what we have read to propel us deeper into the will and ways of our Creator.

This is the goal of the series. The vision is for you to first dig into high-level scholarship that plumbs the depths of biblical history, culture, language, and theology. But you won't just stop there! Next, you will connect the ancient words of the Bible to eternal truths and see how they carry throughout to our modern world today. Finally, the goal is for you to see those eternal truths of God come alive in every part of your life.

Each of the studies in the series is based on The NIV Application Commentary series—one of the most dynamic and well-rounded volumes of commentaries available today. The scholars behind each of these works take readers on a round-trip journey first back to biblical times and then forward to our times today. Along the way, they dig into deep theological insights that bridge the ancient biblical text to the modern world with theological and interpretive integrity.

Prompts have been provided in each lesson of the series to help guide your experience. Each lesson begins with a brief introduction that identifies a key theme for that session. You will then read the biblical text you will be studying. **(Note that these are selected texts and not every passage in the book of the Bible that you are studying may be covered.)** Try to read every passage slowly, thoughtfully, and prayerfully.

Each biblical passage is followed by an **Original Meaning** section, drawn from The NIV Application Commentary series, that will help you understand the author's original intent behind the writing and how the original readers would have interpreted that text. This is followed by the **Past to Present** section, which is intended to help you bridge the gap between the ancient and modern and understand how to connect what you just read to your situation today.

You will find **application and reflection questions** in every lesson to help you in this regard. If you are doing this study on your own, use them for reflection, journaling, and digging deeper into your own growth in faith. If you are walking through this study with a few friends or in a small group, use them for group discussion and interaction.

Finally, at the end of each session is a brief **prayer** prompt. This is designed to be a launchpad into a time of personal prayer around the major theme or themes of the session. Use this prayer as a prompt to help you seek God, gain the understanding that he wants you to have, and discover his power at work in your life.

It will be a great adventure . . . so let's begin!

The Gospel of Mark at a Glance

Author: Although the Gospel does not have an author listed in the text, there is consistent testimony in the early church that John Mark is the author. He was a close associate of Peter, who would have passed on firsthand information about the life and ministry of Jesus.

Date: Many believe the Gospel of Mark was written in the AD 50s or early 60s. Others believe it was inspired and penned later, shortly before the destruction of the temple in AD 70. It is widely accepted by scholars that Mark was the first of the four Gospels to be written.

Setting: Mark likely wrote his Gospel from Rome. The church was facing major crises at the time. Christians had to cope with the death of eyewitnesses, which created the need to conserve the traditions about Jesus. Christians also had to deflect government suspicion of them as a potentially subversive group and defend themselves against religious rivals who could foil the church's growth. Mark's written record of the preaching of Peter thus aided the church's task of proclaiming the gospel throughout the Greco-Roman world.

Focus: The focus of Mark's Gospel is that our faith in Jesus is built on the strong foundation that he is the divine Son of God who came in humility to announce the coming of God's kingdom to our world. Jesus, the Servant King, left the glory of heaven to bring hope, healing, life, truth, and grace to all who accept his message. Mark's Gospel is succinct, unadorned, and vivid. His action is fast-paced in the first half of the book but then slows down in the second half. Mark does this to call our attention to the centrality of the cross for disciples of Jesus. In his Gospel, which can be read aloud in about an hour and a half, we encounter the drama of the unveiling of the Messiah intertwined with the humanity of our Savior.

The Messiah Arrives

Mark 1:1-13, 14-15, 16-45

Writers understand the purpose and the power of *backstory*. It is not enough to just introduce a character into a plot and then carry on from there. No, we want to know what makes that person tick. What happened in the past that shaped his or her nature? What trials has that person had to overcome? What trauma stills lingers that is impacting how he or she thinks and acts?

When this information is missing from a story, we feel a bit shortchanged. It is as if the writer didn't care enough about us as readers to include those vital details! This can be our reaction when we read the opening chapter in Mark. The only real backstory we are given about Jesus, the protagonist in the story, is a prophecy in Isaiah about a messenger who will prepare the way for him. (This messenger turns out to be John the Baptizer). Jesus then suddenly appears "from Nazareth in Galilee" on the shores of the Jordan River to be baptized.

We are given nothing about Jesus' lineage. No notes about Jesus' earthly parents. No mention of the magi, or the star in the east, or the mad king Herod. No angels appear, and no shepherds come to where Jesus is born. The question is . . . *why*? Why does Mark leave out these details that other Gospel writers include? This is a question we will examine in this lesson. Mark had a purpose in leaving out these details. In fact, what he leaves out tells us a lot about Jesus' identity.

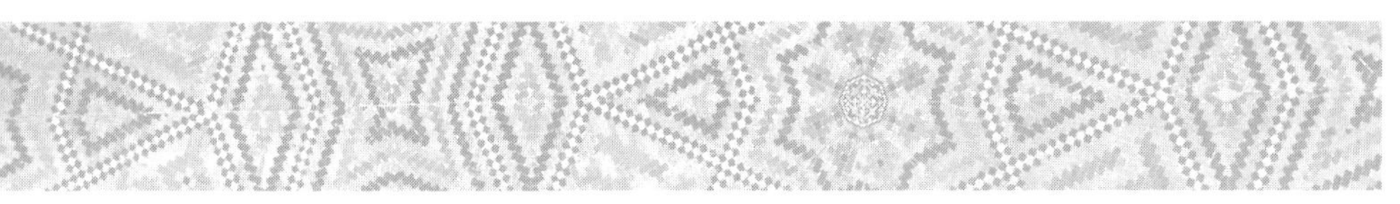

Mark's Prologue [Mark 1:1–13]

[1] The beginning of the good news about Jesus the Messiah, the Son of God, [2] as it is written in Isaiah the prophet:

> "I will send my messenger ahead of you,
> who will prepare your way"—
> [3]"a voice of one calling in the wilderness,
> 'Prepare the way for the Lord,
> make straight paths for him.'"

[4] And so John the Baptist appeared in the wilderness, preaching a baptism of repentance for the forgiveness of sins. [5] The whole Judean countryside and all the people of Jerusalem went out to him. Confessing their sins, they were baptized by him in the Jordan River. [6] John wore clothing made of camel's hair, with a leather belt around his waist, and he ate locusts and wild honey. [7] And this was his message: "After me comes the one more powerful than I, the straps of whose sandals I am not worthy to stoop down and untie. [8] I baptize you with water, but he will baptize you with the Holy Spirit."

[9] At that time Jesus came from Nazareth in Galilee and was baptized by John in the Jordan. [10] Just as Jesus was coming up out of the water, he saw heaven being torn open and the Spirit descending on him like a dove. [11] And a voice came from heaven: "You are my Son, whom I love; with you I am well pleased."

[12] At once the Spirit sent him out into the wilderness [13] and he was in the wilderness forty days, being tempted by Satan. He was with the wild animals, and angels attended him.

Original Meaning

Mark introduces his readers to Jesus, the promised Messiah and Son of God. The first verse serves as the title to the work, informing readers the story he will tell is not a typical one. The remaining verses function as a prologue, through which Mark lets his readers in on certain secrets that will remain hidden to the characters in the drama that follows.

Jesus and John seem to appear out of the blue in Mark's Gospel, but it is clear they arise from the foundation of God's plan for the world. Mark shows their arrival is bound to God's promises in the Old Testament and continue the story of his saving activity. Long before the promise-filled preaching of John the Baptizer, there was the promise-filled preaching of Isaiah.

Mark tells us nothing about Jesus' background, pedigree, or birth. Jesus just appears at the shore of the Jordan River to be baptized by John. Mark says the heavens are "torn open" at the event—a sign that God is about to act (see Ezekiel 1:1). What is opened may be closed, but what is torn cannot return to its former state. The barriers have been removed, and God is now in humanity's midst. We can interpret the voice at the baptism as God's announcement that Jesus has been chosen to rule over his people and that he assumes royal power as king.

The Holy Spirit's descent on Jesus "like a dove" does not induce a state of inner tranquility. Rather, it drives Jesus into the desert and the clutches of Satan for forty days (a biblical round number). The mention of the wild beasts conjures up images of Adam, who also started with the beasts in the garden of Eden (see Genesis 2:19). Satan must now contend with a *new* Adam, who has the power of heaven at his side and angels in his corner.

❖ As you consider the significance of Jesus' identity, what is the significance of God removing the "barriers" between heaven and earth?

____

____

____

____

____

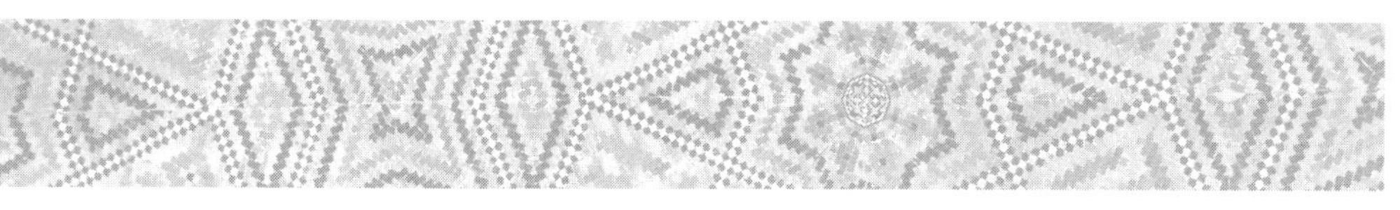

Past to Present

When it comes to determining how this passage applies to us in the *present*, we first have to look at what it meant to the original readers in the *past*. We will discover that there are timeless truths that can guide us today, much as they did in the time of the Bible.

The Wilderness

When Mark was written, Christians were facing persecution for their faith. So Mark wrote his Gospel to remind believers of the foundation on which that faith was built, introducing Jesus as the promised "Messiah" and "Son of God." In the opening scene, John the Baptist appears in the wilderness to announce the Messiah's arrival. In Scripture, the "wilderness" was where God led the Israelites during the exodus (see Exodus 13:18), the place they left to enter the Promised Land (see Joshua 3:1), and where God said he would lead his people back to him (see Hosea 2:14). The wilderness was God's landscape for refining his people.

Just like Mark's readers, we need a refined faith built on a solid foundation. We also need to know there will be times when God will lead us into the "wilderness," just as Jesus was led into the wilderness for testing. As we experience situations that challenge and stretch our faith, we will be compelled to seek God in prayer and discover the truths that he reveals to us through his Word. It is in life's wilderness journeys that we discover our relationship with him has deepened and we have grown in our faith.

❖ How do you know your faith is built on a firm foundation? When have others challenged that what you believe about Jesus is true?

____

____

____

____